love is patient, *love* is kind

love is patient, *love* is kind

A CHRISTIAN
marriage devotional

Rebuild, Reconnect, and Grow in Christ

AARON & APRIL JACOB

ALTHEA
PRESS

Cover and Interior Designer: Emma Hall
Editor: Nana K. Twumasi
Production Editor: Erum Khan

ISBN: Print 978-1-64152-300-4 | eBook 978-1-64152-301-1

To Mark and Terri, Eric and Tina, and Mark and Julie—
our parents and stepparents—who taught us about
true love and new love, as well as the healing, hope,
and help that the Savior can bring to all marriages.

CONTENTS

Beloved, **if God so loved us, we ought also to love one another.**

1 JOHN 4:11

INTRODUCTION

We were married on August 22, 2008, in the Mount Timpanogos, Utah, Temple of The Church of Jesus Christ of Latter-day Saints. That was the most significant day of our lives because it's the day our eternal family unit was formed. That's the day we said yes to each other and yes to God in promising to love and care for one another. On that day, we gave ourselves to each other and agreed to walk hand in hand and side by side through all the adventures of life.

One of the things that made that day so significant was something that was said in our marriage ceremony. Instead of "until death do us part," we pledged "for time and for all eternity." We believe that marriage is ordained by God and that it is intended to last forever. And if our marriages are meant to be eternal, then they are worth our very best efforts.

In 2014, we started the website *Nurturing Marriage* (www.Nurturing Marriage.org), which provides couples with practical and actionable tips to better strengthen their relationships. While it's mostly nondenominational, the tips and advice we share are rooted in our faith in God and Jesus Christ. Along this journey, we've had the privilege of communicating with hundreds of individuals and couples about their relationships and marriages. We've been inspired by countless stories of commitment and sacrifice, and heard many tales of hardship and heartache.

All this is to say: We get marriage. We are in the trenches with you. We're more than a decade into our marriage, and we're still learning, growing, and working to build the kind of marriage we want and the kind of marriage we know God wants for us.

If you've been feeling a little discouraged, depressed, or even desperate regarding the state of your union, this book is for you. It's for those who sometimes feel like they might not have the energy or strength to keep going but don't want to give up. It's for couples who love the Lord and want to keep Him as the center of their marriages, who dream of having more peace, joy, fulfillment, and connection in their marriages.

Please don't think there is anything wrong with you if you and your spouse are struggling with any of the difficult topics this book addresses. You are normal, you are human, and you are not alone. You likely picked up this book because you love your spouse and you love the Lord, and you know that your marriage can be more and better than it is when you let Christ in. Well, you're right, and you're in the right place.

Marriage was meant to turn us heavenward and help us find wholeness and healing together in Christ. Think of it as a triangle with God at the top-center point and you and your spouse each at one of the two bottom points. As you put in the spiritual work necessary to draw closer to God, your faith and spirituality will be elevated, and you'll draw closer to God at the top of the triangle. The amazing thing is that as your efforts move you closer to God, you also draw closer to your spouse.

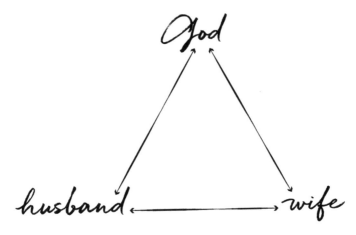

For years now, we've had a special routine in our marriage. Every day, usually before we go to bed, we study the scriptures together side by side. We decided to pursue this routine fairly early in our marriage, and it has been a blessing to us both. Beyond strengthening our individual faith, it has renewed our resolve to keep the promises we made to each other on our wedding day, inspired us with practical ideas for nurturing our marriage, invited us to come unto Christ, and filled us with a joyful perspective about what marriage is and can become with God's help.

We hope this book encourages you to create sacred routines in your relationship as well. It's our goal to help other couples like us feel encouraged, inspired, and hopeful about the marriage that can be theirs and the changes that can happen when God is a part of the marriage relationship. If you're trying to figure out how your marriage can be strengthened, restored, and rebuilt in Christ, we're confident that the scriptures and devotions in this book will help you.

We can't take complete credit, of course. If something touches you, helps you, or encourages you, that is a gift from God. And our interpretations of scripture are strictly our thoughts. We don't claim to know or understand everything about God's Word. But we know we love it, and we've done our best to present stories and passages that will help lift, encourage, and guide you as you strive to come to Christ and let Him help and heal you.

HOW TO USE THIS BOOK

This book contains 52 devotions that you and your spouse can read and ponder together every week of the year. Each devotion provides a Bible passage about important principles to apply to your relationship and marriage, followed by additional stories, quotes, activities, and/or questions to consider.

We've always been big proponents of creating better routines and rituals in marriage. Let studying this book, especially the referenced scriptures, be one of your sacred routines. Carve out time from your schedules to study, learn about, and discuss things of an eternal nature. Creating a spiritual routine with your spouse will build faith, invite connection, and help you keep God and your marriage as your number-one priority.

Just a word of warning: You will get busy. Things will get in the way. Life will happen. And you can bet that Satan doesn't want you two spending this time together focused on practical and spiritual learning and growth. So be patient with yourself if you miss a week. Keep at it. Commit to using this devotional together as a springboard toward the connection, growth, and progress that you both want for your marriage.

You can go through these devotions in order, or you can target certain devotions that are focused on your current needs. Either way, we encourage you to go through the whole book together, even if initially you don't think a certain topic is applicable to your life. You may be surprised by what inspiration, encouragement, and practical tips come from studying certain sections together. Record your thoughts in a journal. The answers to the unasked questions in your heart might come to you, and you might receive direction you didn't know you needed.

We also invite you to sincerely participate in the discussion questions and activities at the end of each devotion; you will get out of this book what you put into it.

Naturally, some of these topics will spark a lot of conversation, and some may bring up feelings of frustration, sadness, or pain. When difficult issues come up, don't be afraid to talk about them. Instead, see them as opportunities to let God help you with your challenges. Pray for ways to talk about them that invite healing. Please recognize that your conversation about a given devotion doesn't need to end after a week. Take the time you need to thoroughly talk through each devotion and the principles it discusses, throughout the week and beyond.

Take time each day to think about what you learned during the weekly devotion, and pray each morning for ideas about how to implement what you're learning in your marriage. As ideas come to you throughout the week, have the faith to follow those nudges and take action. Your marriage will thank you, and you'll find that God can work true miracles within you. You and your spouse may want to begin the next week by sharing something you noticed went well the previous week, or something you learned, tried, or want to do better.

As the year passes and you both use this devotional to help you draw closer to God, we encourage you to keep a record of the great things God does for your marriage. Use a journal or notebook to record small wins, improvements, and miracles in your own relationship.

We hope you know that we, and many others, are cheering you on, trusting that God has great things in store for your union!

May God bless you to develop a sacred intimacy of shared hearts, shared vision, and shared purpose as you work toward the kind of marriage you can achieve through intentional effort and nurturing.

Be of *good comfort*, be of one mind, live in peace; and the God of love and peace shall be with you.

2 CORINTHIANS 13:11

the power of *beginning*

But be ye doers of the word, and not hearers only, deceiving your own selves.
James 1:22

There is great power from God that will come into your life the moment you begin putting His truths into action. Every time you actually take a step forward and *do* something with what you're learning and feeling, you're showing your faith by your works. As you begin to act, move forward, and try, God will help you make progress. He will strengthen, encourage, and empower you. He will guide you along.

Through our more than 10 years of marriage, and in our relationship-coaching efforts with others, we've realized that you don't always learn something until you live it. You won't know the importance of forgiveness until you give and receive it, you won't know how prayer works until you start praying, and you won't know how important romantic time together is until you make an effort to engage in it.

As you experience the process of creating your happily ever after, you'll realize something very quickly: It's hard work! It's not easy to build anything of significance or meaning, and that includes marriage. It takes a great deal of attention, diligence, intentionality, and even a little endurance. But the end result is well worth it!

You'll be tempted to make excuses along the way and to slack off from the hard work necessary to achieve the end goal. But don't give up. Whenever you're creating new habits, routines, and rituals in your life, you have to start somewhere—usually somewhere simple. Enjoy the journey, and keep your focus on the prize. Celebrate the successes along the way, and let them further motivate you to keep pressing forward.

Each devotion in this book will give you a chance to take a step forward in the process of restoring and rebuilding your marriage. What will you do with each new opportunity to act? How will you close the gap between motivation and action? How will you actually begin to make the changes necessary to having the marriage you long for?

First, make truth applicable to you. It's easy to find inspiration—via scripture, faith-based podcasts, talks, and more—but little good comes from the time we devote to those things if we don't apply their lessons to our lives. That can be hard because most of the time we're incredibly resistant to change. So rather than focusing on and getting overwhelmed by the changes you want or need to make, try focusing on the truths you're learning and setting achievable, realistic, and incremental goals.

Second, pray for motivation, strength, and grace. Pray for help taking the small steps necessary to begin to change and improve. Pray for hope, healing, courage, and fortitude.

Finally, just get moving, even if you need to start small. When you don't feel like running a mile, the first 10 steps are the hardest—so just focus on those first 10 steps. Begin walking in the direction you want to go. Begin putting a little extra effort and work into your marriage. Begin having faith in God and putting His promises to the test.

"It has been said that the door of history turns on small hinges, and so do people's lives. The choices we make determine our destiny . . . May we ever choose the harder right instead of the easier wrong."
—Thomas S. Monson

Each devotion in this book will invite and inspire you to act. As you do the things you feel inspired to do, you can have confidence that God will help you with your most important relationship. You'll begin to see how daily habits done on a consistent basis can invite real and positive change that will improve your marriage and transform it into what God intends it to be.

FOR DISCUSSION

○ What blessings have come to you from beginning something hard or uncomfortable in the past?

○ What do you and your spouse need to begin doing together in order to restore and rebuild your relationship with each other and with Christ? What is getting in the way of starting?

○ How will you motivate each other to continue working through this devotional?

○ Read James 2:18. What is one thing you already know you need to do in order to strengthen your marriage?

spending time in God's word

This book of the law shall not depart out of thy mouth; but thou shalt meditate therein day and night, that thou mayest observe to do according to all that is written therein: for then thou shalt make thy way prosperous, and then thou shalt have good success.

Joshua 1:8

It's often been said that when we want to speak to God, we pray, and when we want God to speak to us, we search the scriptures. Studying the Word is an essential practice for any Christian for several reasons.

1. Spending time in God's Word is equivalent to spending time with God. And you can't spend time with God without His influence, love, light, and grace rubbing off on you.

2. Time in the scriptures invites reflection and inspiration regarding personal questions, anxieties, frustrations, and challenges. We all need that.

3. God's Word teaches truth, and obedience to God's truths will guide you in how to live a life full of happiness and connection.

4. God's Word brings healing and power into your life. There is a transformative power found in the scriptures that can be yours if you decide to open them.

5. The scriptures lead us to Christ. They don't just teach of Christ and fill us with Christ's love—they actually help us come to know Him and become more like Him.

There are few habits that will benefit your marriage more than making time in the scriptures a daily habit, both individually and as a couple. In fact, it may be the single most important thing you can do to improve your marriage.

Why?

As you spend time in the scriptures, you'll come to know the Savior, and He will find a place in your heart. In fact, He'll give you a new heart, one that has much more room to love yourself, your spouse, and all those around you. As you invest time in God's Word, your character and disposition, as well as your nature and desires, will change for the better, and so will your marriage. Where once you responded with impatience and contempt, you'll begin to wield greater empathy and compassion. Where once you thought mostly of yourself and your problems, you'll naturally turn outward and focus more on serving your spouse. Where once you filled your day with distractions, you'll now use more of your time to deepen relationships, gain skills and knowledge, and do good in the world.

There is no one right way to study the scriptures, but here are a few tips that help us:

○ Find time to study alone and together each day.

○ Study for time, not for pages, and try to allocate a meaningful amount of time each day.

○ Begin and end with a prayer.

○ Start with a question. As you find answers, ask more questions.

○ Keep a journal and write down your thoughts as you read.

○ Make an action plan. Decide what you're going to do because of what you learn.

○ Live what you learn. Create a pattern of learning, living, and learning more.

○ Be consistent and keep at it. You may not see an immediate change, but that change will come.

Every effort you make to search the scriptures will lead you toward the answers you've been seeking for your marriage by increasing your understanding, filling you with God's love, and helping you find the strength and courage to do the work necessary to build a beautiful, lasting marriage.

FOR DISCUSSION

What can the following verses teach you about the importance of studying God's Word daily?

- 2 Timothy 3:16
- John 5:39
- Acts 17:11
- Romans 15:4

CHALLENGE

Begin keeping a journal when you read the scriptures. Writing will help you slow down, look more deeply at the text and its message, express what you know, and record the direction that God provides for your life.

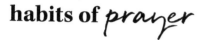

habits of *prayer*

Then shall ye call upon me, and ye shall go and pray unto me, and I will hearken unto you. And ye shall seek me, and find me, when ye shall search for me with all your heart. And I will be found of you, saith the Lord.
Jeremiah 29:12–14

We live in an age of rapid, often instant communication. We have all sorts of apps and devices at our fingertips to talk with anyone, anywhere, anytime. But in order to achieve the marriage you both want, you'll need the only communication tool that draws you closer to God, individually and as a couple. That tool is prayer. Prayer doesn't cost money, will never experience outages, and is always the clearest, fastest way to communicate with the ultimate source of truth and knowledge.

If you'd like to improve the effectiveness of your prayers, recommit to making them a habit and seek to increase their sincerity. Rather than mindlessly reciting the same grocery list of needs day after day, try talking to God like you'd talk to your best friend. He loves you and wants to have a relationship with you. Share with Him all the worries, stresses, desires, hopes, and fears of your heart. Share the drama of your life, the decisions you're trying to make, the solutions you've come up with, what you're working on, and other ideas you want to implement. Ask for His counsel, wisdom, and input—His help, healing, and love.

Then listen. Write down the ideas and impressions that come to you during prayer or throughout the day, and act on those thoughts. They come from God through His Spirit and are personalized instructions for you and your life.

INDIVIDUAL PRAYER

Personal, individual prayer is perhaps the best place to begin because you have complete control over it. Begin by praying both morning and night, and add in any other time when you need an extra boost. Begin your day by thanking God for specific blessings. Tell Him about what you need to do that day, and ask for His inspiration, help, and guidance. At night, your prayers might contain more gratitude, a heartfelt report of the day, and specific details of what you accomplished or what's weighing on your mind.

Prayers can be given in the silent chambers of your heart and mind as you walk down the street or into a meeting. They may consist only of a single word, like "help" or "thanks." Some of the sincerest prayers we've ever offered have been given in moments of great chaos and have lasted only a second or two. You can pray always—during difficult times, good times, stressful times, and lonely times. Pray while you walk, while you drive, while you exercise, and while you work. Pray for whatever you need—even for help learning how to improve your prayers!

PRAYER FOR COUPLES

Developing the daily habit of praying as a couple will strengthen your marriage the moment you begin. Praying together and hearing your spouse pray for you will increase the love and unity in your relationship. Even if you don't feel like praying together, pray.

This habit is ideally implemented when you and your spouse are on the same page and in good standing with each other. That way, when life happens and you have a bad day, the routine is already established, and you have a natural opportunity to address the issue together in prayer and reconcile with each other. With this pattern established, prayer can be an incredibly helpful source of rebuilding and strengthening your relationship after issues or stresses may have brought out the worst in you.

From our experience, praying together after a disagreement has allowed us opportunities for healing as we've held hands and apologized for the way we treated each other, promising again to cherish and nurture each other and our relationship.

FAMILY PRAYER

Just as praying as a couple strengthens the relationship between spouses, praying as a family strengthens the relationships between family members. Gather your family around you and pray together. Say a morning prayer together before you head out the door and go your separate ways. Then, when you've all returned home, say an evening prayer together before you retire for the night. This habit will strengthen your family, give you each the extra support you need to handle the tasks of the day, and fill your home with peace and joy.

Learning to pray often and to recognize answers to prayer will help you become a better individual and, therefore, a better spouse. Not only will you be better able to handle your personal stresses and struggles, you'll also be more in tune with your spouse's needs and specific steps you can take to help them and your marriage.

FOR DISCUSSION

Read the following passages and answer the accompanying questions.

○ What can you learn about prayer from Matthew 6:5–15?

○ Read Matthew 18:20. What does this verse teach about praying together as a couple and/or family?

○ How has praying together blessed you as a couple?

○ What can you do to improve your prayers?

○ How does prayer help you feel God's love for you?

nurturing your *marriage*

He which soweth sparingly shall reap also sparingly; and
he which soweth bountifully shall reap also bountifully.
2 Corinthians 9:6

The law of the harvest is a beautiful law to apply to marriage because,
as Paul explained in the verse for this devotion, what you plant in your
marriage and how you take care of it determines how your marriage
will grow and what you'll get out of it.

Take a look at the kinds of seeds you've planted in your marriage.
You cannot plant seeds of neglect, selfishness, immaturity, and dishonesty
and hope to grow a happy, healthy, and lasting marriage. Instead, you
need seeds of kindness, respect, compassion, selflessness, appreciation,
thoughtfulness, loyalty, trust, and love.

**"God created marriage. No government subcommittee envisioned
it. No social organization developed it. Marriage was conceived and
born in the mind of God."**
—Max Lucado

It's never too late to start planting the right kinds of seeds in your
marriage. You may think it's too late, that your habits are too ingrained,
or that your problems are too difficult to overcome. But nothing is too
difficult to overcome when you have the Savior of the World at your side.
Now is the very best time to tend to the garden of your marriage with
all the diligence and intentionality you can muster, letting the Savior
strengthen, help, and bless your union.

There's nothing more important than being committed to the process. Just as it takes water, sun, and nutrients for plants to grow, it will
take time, space, and committed, intentional care for your marriage to
grow. You have to be loyal and determined, consistent in your efforts day
by day, if you're to reap the reward of a beautiful marriage.

If you implement some of the ideas in this book and don't see changes happening immediately, we urge you not to give up. Every time you try to establish a new habit or gain a new skill, remember that growth, improvement, and progress take time. You won't always see what's happening under the surface all at once. Change happens inside first, and slow growth is good growth. As long as there is upward progress and your marriage is growing, you're on the right track.

Remember, you're not alone in your efforts to nurture your marriage. If you're willing to steadily take care of this precious relationship that is yours day after day, and if you're willing to put in the work necessary to nurture your marriage, then certainly God will support, lift, and bless you in your union. With God as the Master Gardener, time, along with persistent and conscientious effort, will reward you with the sweetest, most fulfilling relationship you can imagine—as Paul promised, a truly bountiful harvest.

FOR DISCUSSION

Read Luke 14:28–30 together and then answer the questions that follow.

- How will a long-term or eternal perspective of marriage change what you do today? How long do you want your marriage to last, and what will you do to achieve that?

- How intentional are you about taking care of your marriage? Is your marriage growing? What do you need to get rid of in order for your marriage to grow in the right way?

- Why are diligence and consistency so important in God's plan of growth for your marriage?

- What is one thing you need to be more consistent about in order to grow your marriage?

- How will you focus on putting more good into your marriage, creating more positive experiences together, and being encouraging and supportive through the process of growing your marriage?

what will *faith* enable you to do?

Who through faith subdued kingdoms, wrought righteousness, obtained promises, stopped the mouths of lions.
Quenched the violence of fire, escaped the edge of the
sword, out of weakness were made strong, waxed valiant
in fight, turned to flight the armies of the aliens.
Hebrews 11:33–34

In marriage and in life, you'll likely encounter a slew of problems, from health challenges and tight finances to problems with children or aging parents and workplace stresses. Sometimes your challenges may seem like mountains—obstacles that cannot be overcome. But with faith, even in the smallest amount, those mountains can be moved. If you want to live a truly meaningful life, overcome your challenges, and build a lasting marriage, faith in Jesus Christ must be your foundation.

Faith is more than just a feeling or a belief. It's action. It's doing more of the things that make you a better person and less of the things that don't, like turning toward your spouse and God when times get rough or turning away from mistakes and past wrongs. It is humbly walking in obedience to God's commandments and trusting in Him. Faith is moving forward, making progress, and working hard, all while hoping for good things to come.

For your marriage to blossom into its full potential, you will need faith in a few things:

1. Faith in yourself to learn, improve, and progress each day.

2. Faith in your spouse and their ability to learn, improve, and progress each day.

3. Faith in Jesus Christ to make it all possible.

While your faith in the first two items may waver from time to time due to natural human imperfections and frustrations, never doubt your faith in item number three. Jesus Christ is perfect and unchanging, and has the ability to help.

How does faith grow? If you're not sure where to start, try these five tips:

1. Read the scriptures.

2. Pray.

3. Repent, forgive, and move forward.

4. Serve others.

5. Follow the Savior and live His gospel.

Each of these activities reminds us of our reliance upon God and fills our hearts with greater love. Faith in Jesus Christ can help you strengthen, restore, and even rebuild your marriage. This is because real, sincere faith leads to action, which in turn invites heaven's help into your life. With increased love and faith, you will see the Savior's hand and influence more and more in your life. His guidance will become a miracle in your marriage, lifting you to higher and happier heights.

FOR DISCUSSION

Hebrews 11 is a beautiful compilation of stories of miracles that were wrought by faith, from Noah to Sarah to Isaac to Moses. Many of these stories begin with two words: "by faith." Take time to read Hebrews 11 with your spouse and consider the following questions:

○ What do you learn about the power of faith from these scriptures?

○ What outcomes are you looking for in your marriage as a result of your faith?

○ How can you exercise faith to achieve those outcomes?

○ What actions will you take as you exercise your faith?

A friend once taught us this powerful application of the examples found in Hebrews 11: "By faith, [insert your names here] were able to [insert your miracle here]."

Here are a few examples of "by faith" statements:

o "By faith, Ryan and Rachel were able to forgive each other and move past their disagreement."

o "By faith, Jenny and Alejandro were able to respond in patience to each other and their children."

o "By faith, Nicole and Cameron paid off $50,000 in debt together."

Write down your "by faith" statement(s), and put it somewhere you can see it often. Then, working backward, create an action plan of steps you'll take—faith steps—to help you achieve the results you're looking for.

learning to *change*

Surely he hath borne our griefs, and carried our sorrows: yet
we did esteem him stricken, smitten of God, and afflicted.
But he was wounded for our transgressions, he was bruised
for our iniquities: the chastisement of our peace was upon
him; and with his stripes we are healed.
Isaiah 53:4–5

If we were to ask you, "What is one thing you wish you could change about your marriage?" what would you say? Would you wish your husband were more patient or that your wife wanted to be intimate more often? Would you wish you fought less or cuddled more? Or would you wish for the transforming power of the Atonement of Jesus Christ to change your heart, even your very character?

If you want your marriage to be better—and who doesn't?—change is not something to wish for but rather something to work toward. The good news is that no matter how difficult your marriage may be, no matter the depth of the problems you're currently facing, the very personal, mostly uncomfortable, and often painful work of change doesn't have to be done alone.

God knows all about your marriage and your marriage problems. He also knows the answers because He is the answer. He ordained marriage, and turning to Him is the only way you can be sure that your marriage will succeed. As you let Him guide you through the sacred process of change, He will help you look inward, turn heavenward, and take responsibility for your choices. You can be different today than you were yesterday, and your marriage can improve in miraculous ways.

Choosing to repent is one of the best things you can do for your marriage because as you let Christ help you change, you'll become a better spouse in the process. Not only will you wake up full of gratitude for the beautiful human snoring next to you, you'll also be less irritated when she spends 50 dollars on a new shirt or when he leaves the toilet seat up. You'll laugh instead of yelling, listen instead of interrupting, and feel less of a need to be right. You'll argue less and validate more, and your communication will be more positive, hopeful, and sincere.

Yes, when you change in Christ, everything about the way you interact with your spouse will change as well. Your heart will open and love will be poured in—a true and pure love for your spouse that comes only when you allow Christ into your heart first. You'll find a closeness, peace, and purpose in your marriage that may have been missing for years.

When you got married, you probably didn't expect it to be such a soul-wrenching, heart-aching, and painfully sacred experience, did you? But that's exactly what God intended marriage to be. He intended for it to change you—or rather, He intended for marriage to turn you to the only true source of change: Jesus Christ.

Please know and remember that it's never too late to make changes, stop doing certain things, and become the person you were meant to be. The power to choose is yours. Also, please remember that change can take time. Sometimes you'll make changes quickly, but more often the changes will take a little longer. However long it takes, you can trust that God is leading you along and that He will help you in your efforts to become more as He is. Your heart will change. Your desires will change. Your actions will change. Your marriage will change—all for the better.

FOR DISCUSSION

- Take a minute to consider the things you're currently doing in your life that make you feel distanced from God. You know what they are. Then take a minute to think about the things you want to be doing in your life (but aren't) in order to feel closer to God. How can you do more of what brings you closer to God and less of what doesn't?

- Think about the things you're doing right in your life. Reflect on how far you've come and who you've become thus far. Commit to continue doing the things that bring you closer to God.

- Reread this week's Bible verse. How can the healing Isaiah mentions come to you? What is required of you?

- Read Romans 6:4 and answer the following questions, discussing together and/or writing in your journal:

  - What does it mean to "walk in newness of life"?

  - How is this possible because of Christ?

  - Are you willing to allow each other the gift of repentance and to help each other walk in newness of life?

  - How has repentance blessed your marriage? How can it do so in the future?

  - How can you know when you have repented and been forgiven?

  - How does understanding repentance help you feel the Savior's love for you personally?

building on *Christ*

Let every man take heed how he buildeth thereupon. For other foundation can no man lay than that is laid, which is Jesus Christ.
1 Corinthians 3:10–11

If you've ever built a new house, you know everything that goes into the process: choosing a plan, signing a whole tree's worth of papers, and then making decisions. Lots of decisions. Then you wait and watch as a foundation is laid, walls are built, and the home slowly starts to come together. Likewise, in your relationship with your spouse, you began by choosing each other, signing a marriage contract to make it official, and then making decisions to build a life together.

Over time, there are all different kinds of problems that a homeowner can run into with the foundation of their home. "Settling"—the subtle shifting or sinking that happens naturally over time—is often normal, expected, and not very costly to fix. Structural damage, on the other hand, can cost a whole lot of money and stress. It requires an expert to determine how bad the damage is, what needs to be done to fix the problem, and if a new foundation needs to be laid.

In any marriage, there are normal conflicts and struggles that are a lot like a foundation settling; they're the kinds of things you'd expect when two are becoming one. But more serious problems arise if the foundation of a marriage is compromised or starts cracking under pressure.

How, then, do married couples create and build on a foundation that will sustain them through the promises they made on their wedding day? The answer can be found in "The Family: A Proclamation to the World," written by modern prophets and apostles and published by The Church of Jesus Christ of Latter-day Saints. This document, which resonates with any Christian denomination, states, "Happiness in family life is most likely to be achieved when founded upon the teachings of the Lord Jesus Christ." No matter the state of your marriage, if you want a happier marriage, family, and homelife, then the foundation to build upon is Jesus Christ.

In order to do that, here are some priorities to focus on.

Gospel study and worship. How can you help your spouse and children (if you have them) draw closer to God? Try implementing or improving family time spent in the scriptures, in prayer, and in worship.

Respect. Pay attention to the feeling in your home and the tone of voice you use with each other. Seek out more positive interactions and fewer negative ones in your relations with your spouse and other family members.

Councils. Make sure to be intentional about having time for family council meetings, couple councils, and one-on-ones with your children. As you take time to talk to your family members and truly seek to understand their needs, God will inspire you with ways to serve and love them better.

Love. If you have children, the best thing you can do for them is to love your spouse. As they see that love and loyalty between you, they will feel safe and secure and will be able to progress in healthy ways.

Fun. Plan fun dates, outings, and trips. Work hard with your spouse and family, then play hard together. The more fun you have together, the stronger the bonds of love, loyalty, and friendship will become.

When you build on Christ, who is the "chief corner stone" (Ephesians 2:20), you will invite peace, love, and healing into your marriage, your home, and your family. No matter what storms or problems arise, He can and will help you build a beautiful life together as you seek to know, follow, and trust Him.

FOR DISCUSSION

Read Matthew 7:24–27 together and then answer the following questions.

- Who is the rock mentioned in verse 25?

- What stood out to you as you read this story?

- Can you draw an analogy from this story to your marriage?

- What other analogies can you make between building a home or foundation and building your marriage?

- How will building on Christ help you when hard times come?

CHALLENGE

Pick one of the priorities listed on page 19 to focus on this week, and pray to know how best to implement it in your life. The Lord will bless you with practical ideas and tips, and as you apply them, the issues you're facing will improve— perhaps more quickly than you even hoped for. It's never too late to build on Christ and to let Him help you overcome and improve.

better *boundaries*

> Whatsoever things are true, whatsoever things are
> honest, whatsoever things are just, whatsoever things
> are pure, whatsoever things are lovely, whatsoever
> things are of good report; if there be any virtue, and
> if there be any praise, think on these things.
> Philippians 4:8

We love football around our house. We love the fans, the passion of the players, and the thrill of the game. We love the strategy, the in-game coaching adjustments, and the creativity so clearly exhibited in "trick" plays. We love the lessons that football can teach about hard work, sportsmanship, and teamwork. If you love sports like us, you know that before the game can begin, the players have to understand the rules of the game. If they don't abide by the rules, or if they try to play outside the bounds of the field, there are penalties—and those penalties make the game harder to win.

In marriage and in life, God has put boundaries in place in order to protect couples and give them a game plan for joy, fulfillment, and success. Unfortunately, in a world that celebrates infidelity and immorality, these rules of the game are often depicted as restrictions that hamper personal freedom and choice. That is simply not the case. In reality, these rules and boundaries are carefully designed by a loving God to help us achieve success and win the ultimate happiness and joy.

In order to be true to your spouse, you need to understand the boundaries that the Lord has set. The Lord expects you to treat your spouse with kindness, respect, love, compassion, and equality. The Lord expects you to be true and completely faithful to your spouse in thought, word, and deed. The Lord expects you to make your spouse's happiness and well-being your highest priority.

Because countless distractions and temptations are out there, it's always wise for you and your spouse to discuss boundaries. Set limits together and help each other—and your marriage—stay safely protected within those bounds. For example, is it appropriate for him to go on a work-related but one-on-one lunch date with a female colleague? Do you feel comfortable with her meeting up with a guy friend from high school who happens to be in town? Do you both want access to each other's e-mails or social media accounts? The answers to these questions are different for every couple, but if you establish them together, you can keep your relationship strong and avoid putting yourselves into tough situations that could cause you to fall outside the bounds.

Finally, the very best way for you to be true to your spouse and honor the boundaries the Lord has set is to follow Paul's counsel in this week's Bible passage and fill your life with goodness. Seek out the things that help you draw closer to God and feel His Spirit. As you intentionally focus your time and energy on activities that nurture and strengthen your marriage, you'll find it easier to be true to your spouse. Your self-control will increase. You'll feel strengthened against temptation. You'll feel closer to your spouse, and your love and loyalty for each other will be a great blessing to you both.

As you prayerfully discuss and apply the boundaries the Lord has set, He will help you see clearly what good boundaries look like and how to protect yourself from crossing them. He will bless you with greater freedom, security, and connection in your marriage.

FOR DISCUSSION

○ How will nurturing loyalty and respect help protect each of you from stepping out of bounds?

○ How can you help each other feel safe and be completely transparent with each other?

○ What boundaries do you currently have in place for protecting your relationship? What other boundaries do you want to put in place?

○ How will boundaries help you feel safe, secure, and free in your marriage? How can they protect against jealousy in marriage?

○ What happens when boundaries are crossed? What can you do if boundaries have already been crossed? How will the gifts of repentance and forgiveness aid you?

the gift of *charity*

Charity never faileth.
1 Corinthians 13:8

As relationship coaches, we understand how important it is to be intentional about making time for our marriage, so not too long ago, we took the opportunity to have a much-needed date night. We dropped the kids off at a friend's house and headed to dinner, but as can happen, it wasn't long before one of us expressed annoyance over something, and the other felt attacked and upset. This wasn't the way date night was supposed to go! It was supposed to be a time to have fun and strengthen our marriage.

We were both tired and stressed, and instead of choosing the high road, we let each other have it. We shared all our frustrations, annoyances, and stresses from the prior few weeks in what was possibly the worst date-night conversation we've ever had. Eventually, we decided to just drive home. We both knew that we wanted and needed to have a nice evening together, but we let pride get in the way, and neither of us chose to be humble and restore the relationship.

After some quiet time to ourselves, God softened our hearts. We realized that we were experiencing growing pains typical of every relationship, especially those going through intense periods of stress and busyness. We also knew that in two hours we needed to pick up our kids, so either we could use this time to be upset at each other or we could try again. We both made the choice to apologize, to forgive, and to use the time we had left to make it a fabulous date. To us, this is what love sometimes looks like. It's a beautiful thing. It grows with time, effort, kindness, thoughtfulness, and a whole lot of sticking it out through thick and thin.

The Apostle Paul teaches us about this kind of love, only he calls it "charity." Review the verse at the beginning of this devotion. Those three little words—"charity never faileth"—have the potential to change your marriage by becoming your go-to answer for most, if not all, of your marital problems.

Charity never fails to be the right answer in marriage because it invites us to think, act, and love as Christ would in every circumstance. Consider that charity is the right answer when . . .

- Your spouse said something that hurt your feelings.
- Your wife is late—again.
- Your husband didn't get you anything for your birthday.
- Your wife broke your trust.
- You're offended by something your spouse said.
- You feel bored with your marriage.
- You feel jealous of your husband.
- Your in-laws say something unkind about you.
- You don't feel sexually close to your wife.
- Disagreements arise about money.
- You're experiencing health challenges.
- You're drowning in stress.

Why do we need charity in marriage? Because it works. As we let Christ into our hearts and our marriages, He works miracles, guides us along, heals our hearts, improves our character, and helps us draw closer to each other. With His help, we can become more like Him and learn to love as He loves, which is essential for building a marriage that will last.

FOR DISCUSSION

○ What does charity look like in marriage?

○ Read 1 Corinthians 13 together and then, in your journal, make two lists: one for what charity is and one for what it isn't.

○ Circle one attribute you feel your spouse exemplifies already. Then star one attribute you feel comes naturally to you. Finally, underline one attribute you want to work on. Share your annotations and thoughts with each other.

○ How can you remember Christ and choose to respond with charity the next time you feel provoked by your spouse? Write down three ways you can respond with charity this week.

○ How can taking time to read from the scriptures help change your heart and fill you with God's love for each other?

Pray for the gift of charity, and then work and act like you've already received it.

learning to *forgive*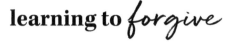

> Put on therefore, as the elect of God, holy and beloved,
> bowels of mercies, kindness, humbleness of mind, meek-
> ness, longsuffering; Forbearing one another, and forgiving
> one another, if any man have a quarrel against any: even
> as Christ forgave you, so also do ye.
> Colossians 3:12–13

It's a good thing the Savior taught us to forgive because forgiveness is necessary and required in order for any marriage to endure the test of time.

When you and your spouse were dating and getting to know each other, you probably could do no wrong in each other's eyes. You focused on the good and gave each other the benefit of the doubt. You exercised patience and cultivated an ability to forgive ahead of time. But soon after the chime of the wedding bells faded, you perhaps started to notice that your practically-perfect-in-every-way spouse actually had a few faults and weaknesses. Not only that, but after sharing bathrooms, beds, and bills, it's likely that moments of frustration surfaced and feelings were hurt.

In those moments of conflict, we should be quick to extend Christlike love and forgiveness, just as we'd hope to receive it in our own moments of fault. As Paul taught the Colossians, when you're faced with the opportunity to take offense and harbor grudges or ill will, you should instead choose to respond with mercy, "even as Christ forgave you."

The institution of marriage is the perfect laboratory in which to practice forgiveness. As you remember your own imperfections and recognize your need for God's grace and forgiveness in your own life, you'll feel more inclined to offer that same forgiveness and mercy to others, especially to your spouse. Forgiveness can come, hurts can be healed, and your marriage can continue on an upward march, but it takes practice and concentrated effort. Doing so can make all the difference in dissipating contempt and strengthening your marriage.

If you've offended or hurt your spouse in any way, big or small, first seek forgiveness from God. Pray to know what to do, what to say to your spouse, and how to change. Pray for courage to be honest and transparent, admit wrongdoing, ask for forgiveness, and apologize. Seek to serve and love your spouse better in order to prove your apology by your changed behavior.

When you're the one who has been hurt, you have the choice to either forgive or not forgive your spouse. While forgiveness is ideally preceded by repentance, your ability to forgive should not be conditional. Forgiveness is just as much for the offended as for the offender. By choosing to forgive and move on, you allow the Savior to remove your hurt.

All of this discussion around forgiveness is not to trivialize the reality that some mistakes have significant consequences and leave lasting scars. In certain circumstances, forgiveness and healing can take an extended period of time. Enlisting the help of close family, friends, or even trained professionals may be necessary. In these painful circumstances, the Master Healer will help you follow His example of extending mercy and kindness.

Remember that it is often very difficult for the spouse who has hurt the other to feel forgiven and loved. Don't hold your spouse's fault over his or her head as a means of control. Don't add to their pain and sorrow by constantly saying, "Don't forget what you did. You're going to be paying for it for a long time."

If you're ready to forgive, then forgive and move on. If you're not ready yet, then keep working toward it. The miracle of forgiveness is not just for you; it's for everyone, including your spouse. As you put your trust in the Savior, you'll be able to leave the past in the past and even forgive your spouse ahead of time for whatever else they may do that hurts you in the future.

Forgiveness is not something you give on your own; it is a gift from heaven that can come to your heart when you are ready and when you seek it. When one spouse chooses to respond to the other's fault with the gift of forgiveness, and when the spouse at fault receives that gift of forgiveness, the marriage is blessed with a new beginning and a fresh start. That is the miracle that Jesus Christ offers to each of us.

FOR DISCUSSION

Read the parable of the unforgiving servant in Matthew 18:21–35 together.

- In what ways have you felt God's love and forgiveness in your own life, and how can you better extend that same love and forgiveness to your spouse?

- Have you sought forgiveness from your spouse for hurts you've caused? Have you said you're sorry?

- What will you do with the gift of forgiveness that you've been given? What is holding you back from offering the gift of forgiveness to yourself and/or your spouse?

- Are you harboring feelings of contempt toward your spouse that are preventing your marriage from progressing? How can you lay these feelings at the Savior's feet and let Him take away the pain and bitterness you feel?

- What is your plan to change? How can you be supportive, patient, and respectful as you allow your spouse the time and space they need in order to forgive you?

- How can you show your spouse that you've forgiven them?

sacred roles to play

Two are better than one; because they have a good reward for their labour. For if they fall, the one will lift up his fellow. Ecclesiastes 4:9–10

God's plan for a husband and a wife to work side by side is a plan of teamwork. As this week's scripture suggests, two are better than one. We each have a different part to play, and sacred roles and responsibilities that are uniquely ours, but never forget that you are working as a team for a greater good.

How do you do that? Here are some tips.

Constantly evaluate roles and responsibilities. Each couple's dynamic is different, and each season of life may require you to reevaluate and/or reassign the various roles that each of you play. We encourage you to regularly meet as companions to review your responsibilities and how you're fulfilling them. Is one spouse trying to carry too heavy a load? Are there ways you can support each other more fully? Some couples never talk about these things and simply expect their spouses to do what they saw their parents do. We don't believe that's the best strategy. If you don't talk about your expectations for how a home will function, then you will run into trouble. Prayerfully consider your current duties, and pay attention to the answers that come. Have the courage to adapt, be flexible, and try new ways of doing things. Working together as a team includes a special interdependence between spouses that builds trust and makes love grow. By evaluating roles and responsibilities together from time to time, you'll be able to enjoy this interdependence regardless of the season of life you find yourself in.

Play your part with joy. No matter what your roles and responsibilities are, your spouse needs you to choose to play your part with joy. It's too easy to wish you didn't have to do the prosaic tasks before you or to wish you could do what your spouse does or what your friend's spouse does. When you recognize how important it is to fill your current role in your marriage/family, and when you see value in what you can offer and bring to that role, you'll be able to play your part with contentment and optimism. Often the joy of marriage comes in the normal, everyday experiences of sharing life with someone. As you try to find meaning in your roles and responsibilities, you'll find that the mundane realities of life can often be sacred experiences that give you the opportunity to turn outward, show love, and serve the people who matter most to you.

Look for ways to support and help each other. Above all, what matters is how you love and support each other in the roles you play. You are equal partners, after all. Be observant and look for ways to bolster your spouse every day. Ask how they're doing, what they might need help with, and how you can share their load. That doesn't mean you always have to be right there working alongside them, but it does mean that you value your spouse's contributions to your family and life together. Express gratitude often. As you show respect and appreciation for the sacred roles your spouse performs each day (and they do the same for you), the power of your teamwork will manifest itself in new and beautiful ways. You'll both begin to recognize that together you can accomplish and become far more than you ever could on your own.

As you and your spouse choose to value each other and respect your current roles and responsibilities, you'll be able to work together in greater harmony and love, and find joy and meaning in the individualized roles you each have to play. You will find that two are better than one, as the scripture says, and that working as a team is the key to creating the cohesive marriage you've always wanted.

FOR DISCUSSION

- Share one thing about your current roles/responsibilities that brings you joy and one thing that weighs you down.

- What changes can you make to your roles and responsibilities that would improve the quality of your relationship?

- What do you each need from the other to feel valued and respected in your current roles and responsibilities?

- Share with each other three things your spouse can do to support you in your roles and responsibilities. Commit to doing one of the things your spouse said this week.

CHALLENGE

Find sacred meaning in your role this week. What opportunities does your role provide you with? What are you learning? How are you serving your family?

choose *peace*

Blessed are the peacemakers: for they shall be called
the children of God.
Matthew 5:9

A few months ago, we'd planned a nice evening at home together. We were having a good time watching a show when, out of the blue, one of us made a comment that rubbed the other the wrong way. That comment triggered another comment, which quickly escalated into a series of comments heading nowhere fast. While we've sometimes let these types of situations spiral out of control in the past, this time we each decided to choose peace over contention. We both humbly recognized our errors, defused the negative feelings, and got back to communicating in healthy ways. It ended up being a great evening!

Occasionally, you and your spouse may say things that hurt each other's feelings. You might be overly critical, impatient, or short-tempered from time to time. This happens to everyone, but if you're not careful, those relatively harmless exchanges can quickly escalate into something far more dangerous.

After more than a decade of marriage, and after coaching many couples, it's become clear to us that most couples' fights start over relatively small issues that somehow get blown out of proportion. The Adversary is a master at fanning tiny flames of disagreement and transforming them into forest fires of contempt, leaving both spouses feeling hurt, alone, frustrated, and empty. Don't let that happen to you. If you've ever gone through or are currently going through a difficult season involving a lot of contention or hurt feelings, please know that things can and will get better as you invite peace in.

Here are a few tips to help you prevent a disagreement from escalating into a damaging event.

o Take a time-out. Give each other a break, go to separate rooms if
you can, and do something else for a while. This will help calm your
emotions and give you the space you need to think clearly and return
better prepared to work through the issue.

o Pray. Say a quick prayer for patience when you want to explode.
Pray to know what a peacemaker would do in the situation.

o Remind each other that you're on the same team. Try saying something like, "We're both obviously getting a bit irritated, but neither
of us wants to fight, so let's just let this one go, okay?"

o Validate each other's feelings. If you show that you recognize and
care about your spouse's feelings, you can defuse tension and quickly
restore peace.

o Laugh. Flirt. Try to break the tension and invite a little humor
back in.

o Give yourself a do-over. If you say something impatient or rude,
immediately correct yourself and apologize: "I'm sorry. I didn't
mean to respond poorly. Let me try that again."

In addition to those in-the-moment tips, here are a few big-picture
strategies to help you avoid negative interactions in the first place.

o Evaluate the demands on your time. Stress kills relationships and
causes more fights than you may realize. Look at your life and try
eliminating a few stressors that are causing more harm than good.

o Take care of your health. If you aren't taking care of yourself by getting enough sleep, eating well, and exercising, your ability to respond
with patience may be hampered.

o Pray to know what to do and how to have more peace. M. Russell
Ballard put it succinctly by saying, "Turn to the Lord in faith and
you will know what to do and how to do it."

- Act on the thoughts that come as you pray. You may feel the need to take your spouse on a date, validate him when he vents about his family, or get up early with the kids so she can sleep in.

- Reach out to trusted friends or trained professionals for counsel and advice. It's nothing to be ashamed of; in fact, it should be encouraged and praised. You'll often find valuable insights that can help increase your peace.

- Accept imperfections. Your relationship will have its fair share of "moments," and that's okay. Don't beat yourself up because you had a bad day. One of the beauties of the gospel of Jesus Christ is that we all have the ability to repent and improve.

The choice to be a peacemaker is yours. As you use these tips to prevent and defuse contention, you'll be filled with a greater abundance of peace in your marriage. That increased peace will strengthen your resolve to continue with these steps, leading to even greater happiness and satisfaction with your spouse.

FOR DISCUSSION

Read the following scripture passages and answer the questions.

- 2 Corinthians 13:11. What does it mean to live in peace? What does it look like?

- 1 Timothy 2:2. What is the peaceable life that God desires for you? Why is peace so critical to a happy marriage? How will choosing to be a peacemaker transform your marriage?

- Ephesians 2:14. What does the phrase, "He is our peace," as used in this scripture mean? How can you let Him break down the wall of partition you may have put up in your marriage?

Ask, and it shall be given you;
seek, and ye shall find; knock,
and it shall be opened unto you.

MATTHEW 7:7

He can *heal* you

He healeth the broken in heart, and bindeth up
their wounds.
Psalm 147:3

Consider this simple observation from the New Testament that may bless your marriage this week: Jesus Christ not only "went about doing good" (Acts 10:38), but He spent a majority of His mortal mission noticing the needs of others, focusing on the one, and offering the miracle of healing to those who would have faith in Him. Jesus Christ worked miracles in the lives of many, and the stories of these miracles live on for us today. These stories remind us that we are not forgotten, that we aren't alone, and that we needn't suffer forever.

A portion of Mark 1 offers a powerful example of Christ's ability to heal. It also expresses a situation common to married couples, this one involving Simon Peter, his wife, and Simon's mother-in-law. This singular experience with the Savior changed their lives forever.

"And forthwith, when they were come out of the synagogue, they entered into the house of Simon and Andrew, with James and John.

"But Simon's wife's mother lay sick of a fever, and anon they tell him of her.

"And he came and took her by the hand, and lifted her up; and immediately the fever left her, and she ministered unto them."
—Mark 1:29–31

There are a few important things to note here:

- The Savior "came and took her by the hand." Figuratively, the Savior will take you and your spouse by the hand as well. He will walk with you on the path toward restoration, healing, and forgiveness.

- He then "lifted her up." The Savior can lift us up, and He will—if we will look to Him and turn to Him, ever ready to follow Him with full purpose of heart.

- "Immediately the fever left her." The Savior healed her. In your life, the healing won't always be as immediate, but it can be. And the miracle is that the moment we let the Savior in, the healing can begin, and often that beginning provides us with all the hope that we need to keep going and to work toward lasting and permanent change.

Why is this story, and similar ones, important to you and your marriage? Imagine how that incredible experience with the Son of God blessed the marriage of Simon Peter and his wife. While it's true that the Savior healed Simon's mother-in-law, this miracle surely gave Simon and his wife an example of the restorative power Jesus could have on their marriage. The same Jesus who healed lives in his time can also heal you and your spouse. He can work miracles in your marriage; He can heal your heart, and He can heal your family.

"Whatever Jesus lays his hands upon lives. If Jesus lays his hands upon a marriage, it lives. If he is allowed to lay his hands on the family, it lives."
—Howard W. Hunter

Jesus Christ knows your struggles, and He can help you. We promise that as you accept His invitation to come unto Him and to let Him heal you and your marriage, you will both feel His love, experience a miracle, and be offered the gift of hearts that have been changed and made whole in Him.

HE CAN HEAL YOU

FOR DISCUSSION

Read and discuss the following scripture and accompanying questions. Then, find ways to apply these passages to your life and to your marriage this week.

○ Matthew 4:23–25—In what areas of your life do you need healing? Do you have faith that Jesus Christ can heal you? Will you let Him symbolically touch your eyes, soften your heart, and strengthen your legs? How will you let Him lay His hands on your marriage?

○ Psalm 107:19–20—How can spending time in God's Word give you immediate access to His healing power? What experiences have you had finding healing as you have studied and pondered the scriptures and the words of God's servants on earth?

○ Isaiah 57:18–19—In the past, how have you seen the Savior's healing come to you in the form of peace and comfort? Will you do the work necessary to allow Him into your life? What is one step you can take this week to invite the Savior into your life so that He can heal you?

prayer *heals*

> Pray one for another, that ye may be healed.
> James 5:16

Everybody talks about the weather. We all notice it, and we're all affected by it. Married life is a lot like weather: Some days are cold, gloomy, and stressful while others are beautiful, sunny, and wonderful.

We've learned that one of the most meaningful and significant resources we have to help us navigate the rain and thunderstorms of married life is heavenly help through prayer. Prayer reminds us that just as the sun is always there behind the clouds, God is still there on dark, difficult days in your marriage. Prayer connects us with heaven and gives us the miracle we need to keep going, to know what to do next, and to make the changes necessary to having a healthy and happy relationship.

When you pray, you can tell God everything and anything—the good, the bad, the ugly, things that seem unfair, and why you feel challenged. As you do this, you'll begin to think more openly, see things more clearly, and feel God's love for you and your spouse. Praying for your spouse, in good times and bad, will fill you with increased love for them. As you pray, you might find that God fills your mind with memories of the kind, generous things your spouse has done for you, big and small. As He does, the challenge of the moment will seem a little smaller, and you'll be filled with a peaceful feeling that only God can give.

"Wherever you are, whatever circumstance you are facing, know that you are not alone in your struggles. God yearns to help you through this journey."
—Jennifer Smith

God will hear you, and He will teach you how to find solutions to your problems and answers to your most heartfelt questions. He will help you understand that things aren't always as they seem and that you should give each other the benefit of the doubt. He will help you glimpse how your spouse might feel. He will help you be humble, look inward, and see your contributions to whatever challenges you might be facing so that you can apologize as needed, repair your relationship, and try, try again. He will also fill you with faith—in yourself, in your marriage, and in the miracles He can work in your relationship.

The best marriage advice you'll receive will come from God Himself through His Spirit. We love the passage in John 14:26 that teaches us of the Holy Ghost's ability to bring all things to our remembrance. So this week, pray to be reminded of the following things:

- Pray that the Holy Ghost will remind you that your spouse is a son or daughter of God. This will help change the way you view and act toward your spouse.

- Pray that the Holy Ghost will help you remember why you fell in love with your spouse in the first place.

- Pray that the Holy Ghost will help you recall all the things your spouse has done right.

- Pray that the Holy Ghost will remind you of Christ and His ability to heal and help your own heart.

FOR DISCUSSION

- How does it make you feel when you pray for your spouse or hear your spouse pray for you?

- Why does God want you to pray during difficult times?

- Why does God want you to pray for each other?

- How will praying for each other and for your marriage invite healing into your relationship?

serving in *secret*

> But when thou doest alms, let not thy left hand know what thy
> right hand doeth: That thine alms may be in secret: and thy
> Father which seeth in secret himself shall reward thee openly.
> Matthew 6:3–4

The bishop of our local congregation once made the observation that
Jesus's Sermon on the Mount in Matthew 5–7 contains some of the best
advice for marriage. The scriptures are powerful because they teach
both doctrine and principles, and those principles can be applied to our
varying life circumstances—including marriage.

One of the best ways to love God is to serve your spouse; for in serving your spouse, you are also serving God. As you can see in this week's
Bible passage, the Sermon on the Mount instructs us to serve "in secret."
What does that mean? In marriage, it could mean loving your spouse—
and putting that love into action—simply because you love them, not
because you're keeping score. You'll probably want your spouse to recognize and appreciate all you're doing for them, and it's good for spouses
to give each other that kind of recognition and appreciation, but what's
most important is that God takes note of all you do.

Serving in secret is more an attitude of the heart than anything else,
and it often looks like small and steady acts of kindness, thoughtfulness,
and love given consistently over time. The key is to do these things, many
of which come naturally, without fanfare or drawing attention to the fact
that you did them.

If you want to improve your marriage, invite connection and draw
closer to your spouse. Start by finding ways to serve your spouse without
thought of reward.

Here are a few ideas to get you thinking:

- Pray for your spouse's goals, hopes, and dreams to be realized.
- Pray to see ways to serve that you might not have considered "service" before.
- Get up early with the kids so he can sleep in.
- Fill her car with gas to save her the time.
- Listen to the podcast he sent you, even if you feel you're too busy.
- If she expresses how stressful her day was, hug her tight for a few minutes.
- Text him to see how his day is going.
- Listen to her and look into her eyes (not at your phone) while she talks.
- Express gratitude to your spouse for small things.
- When you're out to dinner with friends, share something you love about your spouse in the course of the conversation.
- Ask, "What can I do to help you?"
- Thank your spouse after making love and tell them what you enjoyed most.
- Take her for a walk and hold her hand the whole time.
- Validate his feelings when he vents about his boss.
- Don't keep tabs on how many girls' nights out she's been on.
- Volunteer to run errands.
- Let him pick the show you watch.
- Pack her lunch every day before she leaves for work.
- Take care of the bills you promised you would take care of.
- Plan a date night he would love.
- Don't nag about what you normally nag about.
- Rub her shoulders.

○ If she's been wanting to get up early together, happily get up early.

○ Offer words of encouragement often: "Good work." "You're a genius." "I knew you could."

As you learn to serve without need for reciprocation from your spouse, you will truly serve humbly, with a pure heart, showing God how much you love Him in the process.

FOR DISCUSSION

The Sermon on the Mount is an invitation to become more like Jesus Christ, to take upon ourselves His nature and attributes. What will you do with that invitation? Read Matthew 5–7 together and then answer the following questions:

○ What can you learn about marriage from the Sermon on the Mount?

○ What truths stand out to you?

○ Why do these truths matter so much?

○ What truths can you apply to your marriage this week?

○ How will applying these principles help you draw closer to God, become more like Christ, and be filled with inspiration about how to nurture your own marriage?

CHALLENGE

Decide to do something to serve your spouse this week, using the discussion points or your own ideas. Serve quietly, humbly, and with a desire to show love for your spouse. Pay attention to how you feel and how your love for your spouse grows when you think of them instead of yourself. You'll notice your heart changing, developing, and becoming more Christlike as you strive to serve and love as the Savior does.

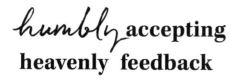

humbly accepting
heavenly feedback

> He hath shewed thee, O man, what is good; and what doth the Lord require of thee, but to do justly, and to love mercy, and to walk humbly with thy God?
> Micah 6:8

Once, Aaron didn't like the way April said something, and he shared his feelings. April took it as correction and didn't like it at all. She walked out of the room, saying out loud to herself, "He's difficult sometimes!" The Spirit whispered right back at her, "*You're* difficult sometimes!" She stood corrected and humbled. It's never easy to receive guidance or correction if we're proud, but if we can be humble, it can make all the difference in our lives.

There is much to learn from the simple story told in John 21:1–14, when the resurrected Savior appeared to his disciples while they were fishing. They didn't recognize Him from their boat as he stood on the shore, and when he called out to ask if they'd caught anything, they said they hadn't. He told them, "Cast the net on the right side of the ship, and ye shall find." They did so—and caught so many fish that they couldn't even lift the net. John immediately said to Peter, "It is the Lord."

How often in your marriage are you like the disciples, doing what you've always done, not recognizing that the Savior of the World stands ready to help you get the results you want? It takes humility to realize there may be a better way of doing things or that you may be a bigger part of the problem than you thought.

The Savior invites you to "cast the net on the right side" in your marriage, too. This is an opportunity to try something new—to rethink how you've been doing things and aim for better results. We like to call this "heavenly feedback." God will inspire you with the right thing to say, nudge you if the way you respond isn't productive, or give you an idea of something you can do for your spouse. At times, the Spirit will clearly whisper something as specific as "cast the net on the right side," while at other times you may just feel a gnawing desire to overcome a specific weakness or do something to lift your spouse up.

Heavenly feedback can also come from your spouse. If they suggest something in a Christlike way that may help you or your relationship, then your spouse may be offering you heavenly feedback. If following your spouse's counsel will help you draw nearer to Christ or become more like Him, then it would be wise to apply that specific counsel and see if you get better results.

We have seen firsthand couples who were humble enough to make hard and lasting changes to save their marriages. We have seen the humility it takes to show up for your spouse, to recognize where you went wrong, to apologize, and to really work on improved behavior (even when your spouse is also at fault). We have seen the humility it takes to seek forgiveness, rebuild trust, and admit that your spouse has a strength or way of doing things that you could learn from.

As you choose to humbly respond to heavenly feedback and have faith in Jesus Christ, He can turn your weaknesses into strengths. He will also guide and mentor you as you seek to become the best version of yourself that you can be and as you work to improve and take care of your marriage. We know that as you choose to follow and apply this pattern of heavenly feedback, you will draw closer to God, grow in confidence, and receive specific inspiration that will bless your marriage this week.

FOR DISCUSSION

- Read John 21:1-14 aloud with your spouse. What can you learn from the humble way the disciples in the story received correction? What happened when they followed the counsel of the Savior?

- When was the last time you received genuine feedback? What was the correction? How did it make you feel? What have you done about it?

- What do you feel you need to change in order to draw closer to God and build a better marriage?

- What is one of your weaknesses that may be getting in the way of having your "marriage net" filled with love, connection, and meaning?

- Why are faith and humility necessary in order to change and overcome weaknesses?

- What miracles can be brought about in your life when you're willing to learn from your spouse and from God instead of stubbornly thinking your way is always the right way?

FURTHER READING

Ponder the following scriptures together with your spouse and talk about the power Christ has to help us change.

- 2 Corinthians 12:9–10
- Matthew 19:26

be of good *cheer*

These things I have spoken unto you, that in me ye might have peace. In the world ye shall have tribulation: but be of good cheer; I have overcome the world.
John 16:33

We live in a world where all things truly are in commotion. Many people are weighed down with anxiety, depression, fear, insecurity—and the list goes on. You may be experiencing similar feelings in your marriage. Perhaps you're struggling personally, your spouse is weighed down with discouragement, or your marriage feels like it's crumbling beneath your feet. The hurt, angst, and frustration that fill your mind and heart may feel all consuming, and the answers and help you've been seeking may feel distant and unachievable.

Let us take the liberty of changing one word in this week's scripture in order to make it more immediately applicable to married life. "In [marriage] ye shall have tribulation: but be of good cheer; I have overcome the world."

How can you be of good cheer in the midst of a chronic illness, a spouse who's been dealing with a significant addiction, or a retirement that was insufficiently saved for due to poor spending habits or debilitating debt? How can you be of good cheer if you feel neglected by your spouse or if they're unwilling to open up and engage in conversation?

When you agreed to marry, you also signed up for growth and progress. None of that is available without struggle, adversity, and some growing pains. Tribulation—aka "hard things"—is part of the package. While they can be very uncomfortable, challenges are normal, and they have great purpose in God's plan. Some things are actually meant to be too hard to face on your own—they present you with the opportunity to turn to God and come to know His love and kindness firsthand.

No matter what is weighing you down or causing you to feel discouraged, the Savior invites you to be full of hope and to rejoice. He overcame every difficult or painful situation you or your spouse will ever face in this life. He felt what you are feeling. He overcame the obstacle in front of you. He knows what to do to help you. Because of who He is and what He has done for you, He can invite you to be of good cheer, and He can show you how to live a joyful life.

As you turn heavenward for help with the things that weigh you down, God will help you navigate the difficult times and be optimistic about your life, your marriage, and your future. He overcame the world, and in Him you will find peace. As you place your fears, anxieties, and worries on Him, He will strengthen you, bless you, and fill your life with more light, hope, happiness, and meaning than you knew possible. He alone can work that kind of miracle in your life and in your marriage starting this very week.

FOR DISCUSSION

- What is weighing you down? How can the Savior help lift your heavy burdens? What can you do for each other to make those burdens feel light?

- What lessons have you learned from the hard things you have been going through? How have you grown through these trials?

- Share your thoughts, feelings, and testimony of the Savior with each other.

- Write down the verse from John 16:33 on a sticky note and put it someplace where you will both see it every day this week.

FURTHER READING

How can the following passages help you focus on the joy found in Christ instead of on any difficulties you currently face?

- Matthew 9:2
- John 15:10–11
- Philippians 4:4

when trust has been *broken*

> Trust in the Lord with all thine heart; and lean not unto thine own understanding. In all thy ways acknowledge him, and he shall direct thy paths.
> Proverbs 3:5–6

Your spouse wants to be true to you. And you want to be true to your spouse. And you both ought to do everything in your power to be true to each other. But what if you find yourself in the middle of a relationship hurricane where trust has been compromised? As unfortunate as it is, life happens, and people make mistakes. We in no way condone poor decisions or violations of trust, but we do acknowledge that they are common occurrences.

For whatever reason, one or both of you may have lost confidence in each other. It may be that you lied about something. Or your spouse hid something from you. Or you aren't fully disclosing everything you should. It may have to do with money, another relationship, or any number of personal challenges or bad choices. It may simply be hundreds of small things that have compounded over time.

Regardless, don't let your spouse's violation of trust cause you to stop trusting the Lord. In fact, trusting the Lord when trust has been broken is one of the best paths forward to hope and healing. Rather than letting a trust-breaking discovery shatter your faith in God, turn to Him for help, comfort, and guidance.

Trust takes years to build and only a moment to destroy. When trust is compromised, it can cause painful and lasting damage. Try to begin rebuilding trust as soon as possible. How? Make the commitment to yourself to be honest and true, and be uncompromising in keeping it. Trust will grow as you keep your word, look beyond yourself to serve others, and consistently do the little things that build confidence. It will take time, significant effort, and intentional dedication, but it will be worth it.

Here are a few practical tips to help you as you work to rebuild or strengthen trust.

To the spouse who compromised trust and is seeking to regain it:

o Draw closer to God. Make scripture study, prayer, and personal worship daily activities.

o Acknowledge what you've done wrong and how you've hurt others.

o Apologize to and seek forgiveness from your spouse. Remember, even if your spouse forgives you, that isn't the same as restoring trust.

o Do everything you can to make restitution for your actions.

o Seek outside help, accountability, and support from trained professionals and clergy as appropriate.

o Keep your promises. Be where you say you'll be. Do what you say you'll do.

o Set clear boundaries and honor them.

o Work on connection and build from the ground up.

o Be patient. Give your spouse the space and time they need for healing.

o Pray for your spouse and your marriage.

To the spouse whose trust was compromised:

o Draw closer to God. Make scripture study, prayer, and personal worship daily activities.

o Don't blame yourself or beat yourself up. Remember that you're not responsible for your spouse's choices.

o Seek support and help from professionals or trusted friends.

o Find forgiveness. While it can be extremely difficult, it's as much for you and your healing as it is for your spouse.

o Acknowledge and celebrate improvement.

- Don't fall into the trap of feeling the need to retaliate.
- Take care of yourself. Do what you need to do to maintain and strengthen your physical, emotional, and spiritual health.
- Be patient. Change takes time.
- Avoid holding the violation of trust over your spouse's head and bringing it up over and over.
- Pray for your spouse and your marriage.

If and when trust is lost, choose to trust God. Turn to Him to better understand what you have to learn and how you can come out stronger. Seek the help you need from trained professionals, and work toward reestablishing trust and confidence.

The Savior can help you rebuild trust, and as you build on Him as your foundation, He can heal your hearts and help make your marriage stronger than ever before.

FOR DISCUSSION

- Are there unresolved issues of trust in your relationship? How can you address those in a healthy manner?
- If trust has been violated, are you receiving the professional help and support you need?
- How can you create a safe environment to be vulnerable and honest with each other?
- What actions will help you show love for your spouse as they choose to disclose personal challenges with you?
- How can you strengthen the trust in your marriage?

what of *time*?

As the one dieth, so dieth the other; yea, they all have one breath.
Ecclesiastes 3:19

At the end of each year, we usually find ourselves reflecting on how quickly the year has passed—even quicker than years previous. We each are given the same 24 beautiful hours in a day. What we do with those hours is up to us. If you want to enjoy a healthier and happier marriage, then pay careful attention to how you allocate your time across your many competing priorities.

You may have noticed that one of the major pulls on your time is also a trend that seems to be taking over relationships around the world. It's a new kind of marriage, really—between humans and their technological devices. We often reach for these devices first thing in the morning and hold on to them until we sleep at night, giving them our undivided time and attention—and leaving more important personal relationships with the leftovers. It's a relationship everyone seems to be in, but it isn't two-way, and it isn't healthy.

Now, there is certainly a time and a place for technology, and we are confident that it has a purpose in God's plan. You can connect with your spouse and family at all times, even extended family and friends. You can literally hold the scriptures in your pocket and take them with you everywhere you go. However, we're confident that God never intended for us to sell all our precious time to these devices.

At the end of your life, there will come a day of reckoning when you stand before God and account for your choices. Who or what got your time? What did you do with all that you were given? How did you care for your most important relationships? You want to be able to say, "Look at what I was able to do with my time, my talents, my resources. See how my priorities were clear by the way I invested my time? This is what I learned, and this is how I overcame great struggles and challenges. With the Savior's help, this is who I have become.

The Adversary would have you squander your time and get caught up in distraction after distraction, diverting yourself from what really matters. He doesn't want you to be happy or make progress in your life. He doesn't want you to realize what a gift your time is. Don't fall prey to his antics.

God, on the other hand, provides you with encouragement, strength, and guidance for how to best use the time, talents, opportunities, relationships, and resources you've been given to grow, progress, learn, change, and give more to others. Your time is precious. You can choose to spend it any way you'd like, but you'll never go wrong by investing it in your marriage and family.

As you pray about how the Lord would have you invest your time, seeking His guidance about how to help your marriage grow, ideas will come to you, and you'll know what to do. We are confident that as you give your *best* time to your spouse and not to other distractions, your marriage can and will thrive, and you two will enjoy greater connection, peace, and joy together.

FOR DISCUSSION

Read the parable of the talents (Matthew 25:14–30) together. Discuss the lessons you draw from this parable about your own life and marriage. What will you do differently this week because of what you learn?

Consider how you spent your time yesterday and ask yourselves the following questions:

- Who got the majority of your time yesterday and why?
- Are you okay with that? How do you feel about it?
- How can you retain more control over where your time goes each day?
- Do you intentionally prioritize your spouse or give them only leftover time?
- How can you put your marriage first instead of last?
- How can you intentionally invest your time in your marriage (making time to talk daily, planning weekly dates and regular getaways, etc.)?

CHALLENGE

Give your spouse one extra hour of your time this week. You can do it all in one chunk, or you can break it up. Put your phone away, turn off the television, come home early from the office. Do whatever you need to do to give your spouse a little more of you by giving them more of your time.

walk with God

> And this is love, that we walk after his commandments.
> This is the commandment, That, as ye have heard from
> the beginning, ye should walk in it.
> 2 John 1:6

Sometimes, we struggle in life and in our relationships because we're walking in the wrong direction, or down the wrong path, or with the wrong crowd. Often, all it takes to get the dying embers of a struggling marriage rekindled is to evaluate who you're walking with and where, and to let God put your feet back on the path that leads to happiness and fulfillment. We all need someone to walk through life with us, and God is the perfect person for the job.

Throughout the scriptures, we see this invitation to walk with Him in one form or another. For example, Isaiah 30:21 reminds us that God will show us the way to walk if we listen to His voice through His Spirit: "And thine ears shall hear a word behind thee, saying, This is the way, walk ye in it, when ye turn to the right hand, and when ye turn to the left." If you take the time to be still and listen to His voice, you will learn how to walk with Him.

You can choose to walk with God, to walk with your spouse, and to walk through life full of faith and hope for a happy future. You can walk with Him through the good times and the bad as you do the things He would do, ministering to your spouse in love and selflessness—listening, empathizing, encouraging, and cherishing.

Here are three practical tips to help you strengthen your relationship with Christ and with your spouse by learning to walk with God.

Counsel with God. God is the perfect counselor because He understands. He knows where we have come from, what we struggle with, what we desire, and where our strengths lie. We simply have to be humble and sensitive enough to follow His advice. In order to counsel with God, pray to Him and talk to Him. Imagine He's sitting right there listening to you. Open your heart to Him. Share your thoughts and concerns with Him. Then listen for answers.

Honor the Sabbath and go to church. Use the Sabbath as a time to turn all your thoughts, energies, and worries heavenward. Keeping the Sabbath is the perfect way to have one day that's different from all the rest—a day that truly renews you and helps you draw closer to God. On the Sabbath, you may choose to enjoy your family's company, study the scriptures, and/or talk with your spouse about things you'd like to do better. Another way to honor the Sabbath is to regularly attend church together. If you're already a churchgoer, consider deepening your commitment to fully participate in your church services. Being around people of faith can strengthen your own faith. You can learn from their examples, be inspired by their stories, and find friends and mentors to help support you.

Serve others. Christ "went about doing good" (Acts 10:38), and we would be wise to follow His example. When we serve others, a beautiful—even miraculous—thing happens. As we focus on the needs and hardships of others, our own struggles that seemed so consuming and burdensome seem to fade away. While service certainly doesn't make our own problems magically disappear, it does put them in perspective. In many cases, we realize that the challenges we face are opportunities for growth, and we find the strength to overcome.

As you walk hand in hand with God and with your spouse through this marriage journey, He will not leave you alone. He will strengthen you, encourage you, and give you the time and skills you need to build a happy relationship.

FOR DISCUSSION

- Read 1 Kings 8:23 and reflect on the promised blessings that have come to you as you've chosen to walk with God.

- Pray with your spouse and have your very first marriage counseling session with God. Write down any ideas that come to you, and try your best to implement them.

- Study Isaiah 58:13–14 together. Discuss why the Sabbath is important for you and what you want the day to look like in your home.

- Commit to going to church this week and discuss how both of you could be more active participants there.

choosing patience and *flexibility*

Tribulation worketh patience; And patience, experience;
and experience, hope.
Romans 5:3–4

We celebrated our 10-year anniversary with a trip to London. As we
started planning, looking at various touristy options, Aaron told April that
one of his must-see attractions was Windsor Castle. April, wanting to do
something a bit more experiential, booked a package tour to see Windsor
Castle, Oxford University, and Stonehenge. It was a great plan that we
were both excited about, and the tour was set to begin at 8:00 a.m.

Well, life happened. We were delayed the morning of the tour. It was
already 7:30 a.m. by the time we set off. But we successfully made our
way to Buckingham Palace and were feeling pretty confident . . . until we
realized we couldn't find the station. We began to run through the streets
of London, checking our map and asking people for directions. April
kept seeing large tour buses and running ahead to catch them, but every
single time we thought we had found our stop, we realized we were in the
wrong place.

When we finally arrived at the correct location, it was 8:10 a.m. We
were red-faced and sweating, and April was nearly in tears as we were told
that our (expensive) bus tour had departed nine minutes earlier, and there
was nothing we could do about it. We asked if we could get our money
back, but unfortunately we couldn't; our lateness was our fault, after all.

In moments of frustration like this, there's a natural tendency to place
blame. But whose fault was it? Aaron could have spent the day mad at
April for not looking up directions because she thought she knew where
she was going. April could have been mad at Aaron for making us late in
the first place. But Proverbs 14:29 teaches the importance of being "slow
to wrath." Although it's often no small task, if we choose to be patient

and flexible and go with the flow, it becomes much easier to remain calm when things don't go our way or when circumstances don't live up to our carefully curated plans or expectations.

Thankfully, the tour company offered to place us on another tour that was about to depart for Bath and Stonehenge. We decided that this was a chance for us to make the best of a situation that hadn't turned out as we would have liked. We both decided not to worry about who was at fault, and we instead chose to love the experience that was before us.

And you know what? We had a great time! The choice to be flexible and optimistic enabled us to create a day full of joy, adventure, and connection instead of irritability, impatience, and blame.

In marriage, it's common for events to get in the way of what we'd hoped, expected, or planned. In those moments, we can choose to be upset, bitter, and angry, or we can choose to be grateful, laugh about it, and make the most of it. There will probably be dozens of opportunities for you to be flexible in your marriage this week. Each one will provide you with the chance to take a step back and be patient or to get irritated and upset. The choice is yours.

As you work to become more flexible and patient, you'll find that these normal life situations provide some of the best opportunities for connection and growth and that your marriage will be better because of them.

FOR DISCUSSION

- In what ways can you be more flexible about day-to-day life and the expectations you have for your marriage and your spouse?
- What other qualities and attributes will you develop as you practice being flexible?
- What expectations do you have for each other and for your marriage? Which are healthy and which aren't?
- What can you do to help each other remain flexible and easygoing when you would normally be upset and frustrated?

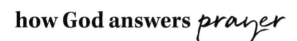

WEEK 22:

how God answers *prayer*

> If any of you lack wisdom, let him ask of God, that giveth
> to all men liberally, and upbraideth not; and it shall be
> given him.
> James 1:5

We love this passage from the book of James. It contains both an invitation and a promise from God. God is inviting you to take your questions, problems, and concerns to Him, to ask Him for guidance, answers, encouragement, and even love. God promises that He won't hold back but that He will give you the answers you're looking for—freely!

You and your spouse are currently facing your own unique set of circumstances. Whether you're in a great season of life or a more difficult one, there are undoubtedly questions you're grappling with, decisions you need to make, or challenges you're facing. You may feel emotionally distant from each other or hurt by something the other has said. You may be stressed about finances or unsure how to handle a problem with one of your children. You may even be experiencing a crisis of faith.

When we find ourselves facing the circumstances life has dealt us, we can take courage in knowing that we have a direct line of communication to heaven. What questions do you need answers to? What problems do you need solutions to? What direction do you need in order to move forward?

God wants you to humbly seek His counsel and guidance, express your desires, explain your reasoning, and tell Him what decisions you have made. When you take your questions, concerns, problems, and heartaches to the Lord, He will hear you. And He will answer you.

He will always hear your prayers, but sometimes recognizing His answers can be a little challenging. It takes practice and a degree of spiritual maturity—something we're all working on developing and strengthening. While God can and does speak to each of His children differently, He usually responds through the medium of the Holy Ghost, who speaks to both the heart and the mind. You may recognize God's answers to your prayers through the following ways:

1. **Feelings that come to your heart.** It may be a feeling of confidence and peace, letting you know that your path is correct and in line with His plan, or it may be a feeling of hesitancy and uneasiness, letting you know that a course correction would be best. When you experience these feelings, be careful not to simply dismiss them as "your own." If you've been praying about whether to take that job in a new city and you've been feeling very uneasy, then learn to trust your gut. It is most likely God speaking to you and answering your prayers.

2. **Thoughts, words, or ideas that come to your mind.** Like the "still small voice" Elijah heard in 1 Kings 19:12, you may feel or hear words in your mind confirming logical conclusions or giving you a specific action to take. The ideas that come to you as you go about your daily tasks, while also making time to quiet your soul and search the scriptures, will often be clear to you, and you will be able to act on those answers with confidence. At other times, the thoughts and ideas that come to you may seem unrelated to your question but shouldn't be ignored. They are often the very answers you have been looking for. As you trust God and listen to Him, your ability to recognize answers to prayer will grow.

Sometimes God won't provide you with direct and specific answers. Instead, He'll expect you to perform the work necessary to seek knowledge and make the best choice you can. While it can feel frustrating not to receive a specific direction, you can take it as a sign that God trusts you and wants you to learn how to make decisions for yourself. You can also rest assured that God won't let you make a significant decision incorrectly without trying to warn you first. So when you encounter these "non-answers," take courage, move forward in faith, and make a choice. Further direction will always come.

Seek to know and do the Lord's will, even if it isn't what you initially would want or expect, because God wants the best for you—and you can't possibly do any better than that! As you do His will, you'll come to recognize the wisdom behind that guidance, and you'll enjoy not just the "good life" you envisioned for yourself but the "best life" that God wants for you.

FOR DISCUSSION

○ Share with each other how God has answered your prayers in the past and how you came to know the answer you received was from Him.

○ What are two things you can take to God in prayer this week? What will you do with the answers that come?

○ What examples from the scriptures do you know of where God answered prayers? Begin by reading Luke 1:13, 1 Samuel 1:27–28, and 1 Samuel 2:21. What can you learn from these stories, and how do these passages apply to your life?

FURTHER READING

○ 1 John 5:14–15
○ James 5:13–18

seasons of marriage

> To every thing there is a season, and a time to every
> purpose under the heaven. . . . A time to break down,
> and a time to build up. . . . A time to love, and a time to
> hate; a time of war, and a time of peace.
> Ecclesiastes 3:1, 3 & 8

Fall has always been our favorite season of the year. We love the colors, the corn mazes, the apple picking, the football games, and the fun holidays. We always feel a little sad when the dark days of winter roll around—although, thankfully, we also enjoy a good snowstorm and the sledding that inevitably follows. Around the end of March, we're looking forward to coming out of hibernation and enjoying a little more sunshine and daylight. When June arrives, the pools are opening, school is closing, and we're ready for some vacation time. Then, before we know it, we're back to the leaves turning colors, and the cycle repeats itself.

In over a decade of marriage, we've learned that life and marriage also have their seasons. Some seasons are busy and exciting while others may feel long and dreary. Some are difficult and stressful while others are bright and cheery. There are seasons when you and your spouse are clicking on all cylinders and nothing can get between you, and there are seasons when tensions are high and you seem to be going at each other every other day. There might be tearful moments when you look at each other and wonder, "How are we still together?" Hopefully, there are many more moments when your hearts are full of gratitude for the blessing of your companionship.

No matter your situation, you're currently navigating one of life's seasons. It might be a season of infertility or a season of chaos as you raise children, of caring for aging parents or of celebrating new grandchildren. It might be a season of pressing demands and significant responsibility or a season of loneliness and lack of purpose, of conflict and stress or of peace and joy.

When the challenging seasons of life and marriage settle in, remember that they won't last forever. You can navigate those gloomy seasons, choose to face them with fortitude, and emerge better and stronger than ever before!

These seasons have a purpose. Even when they're caused by poor choices or selfishness from you or your spouse, they can still teach you important lessons to help you grow. For example, these challenges often remind us of the following truths:

- You always have a choice. The challenging experiences you face individually and as a couple can either soften or harden your hearts. What will you choose?

- You can't do life or marriage alone; you need each other, and you need God.

- God often uses trials to teach and refine us. There are certain lessons and experiences you need in order to grow into the type of people God wants you to be.

- There is power in unity. Trials can be a galvanizing force, uniting you in a common cause and making you stronger than ever.

For those in the thick of hard times, don't give up. Ecclesiastes 3:11 says, "He hath made every thing beautiful in his time." If you turn to God for help during your season of trial, every challenge you face can be for your benefit and growth. With His help, your season of hardship in marriage will also pass, and a beautiful new season will unfold before you.

FOR DISCUSSION

Read Ecclesiastes 3 together, then answer the following questions:

- What season of marriage are you in right now? What is the best thing about the season you're currently in?

- What is the hardest thing? What lessons are you learning in this season?

- How can you make this season great?

turn your hearts to your *family*

And he shall turn the heart of the fathers to the children,
and the heart of the children to their fathers.
Malachi 4:6

Whenever we have birthdays in our family, each person wakes up to
decorations, presents, and a fun breakfast—and also a bowl turned
upside down on the table. It's a family tradition called "birthday quarters." Under each bowl is a quarter for each year the birthday boy or
girl has been alive. So our nine-year-old had nine quarters under his
bowl this year, our six-year-old had six, our two-year-old had two, and
. . . we won't mention how many quarters we each get under our bowls.
Birthday quarters is a tradition brought into our marriage from Aaron's
family. His parents did it with their kids, and his grandparents did it with
their children. We thought it was simple, meaningful, and special enough
to carry into our family and make it one of our traditions as well.

God's plan is all about families, and in His plan, families are forever.
While no two families are the same—they may differ in culture, language,
stage of life, and a hundred other things—God's promises extend to them all.

Marriage is the coming together of two unique individuals to create
their own new family unit. As that union of two families occurs and
a new family unit is born, it's common to experience growing pains.
Marrying into a new family often causes some drama. You may not
always feel included or welcomed. You may feel judged or controlled.
You may not enjoy spending Christmas in your spouse's little brother's
bedroom, and sometimes your in-laws may feel more like out-laws.

But regardless of these challenges, you're still family. No matter how
difficult your extended family or in-laws may seem, with the Lord's help
and a little patience, you can learn to love them and be there for them,

just like family should. You might even inherit some beautiful traditions, like birthday quarters.

Here are some suggestions to help you turn your heart toward your extended family.

Be a team. No matter the situation, whether you're visiting his parents' home or her mother is coming into town for the next two weeks, remember that you two are a team first. You are your own family unit, and you can overcome any difficulties with your respective family situations when you think of your spouse and their needs and feelings first. Respect each other and stand up for each other. Your priority and loyalty should be to your spouse first and your extended family second.

Appreciate. Be grateful for the role your extended family has played in the amazing person your spouse has become. Remember how central and important families are in God's plan and how beautiful and powerful an influence they are in your life. No family is perfect, so rather than focusing on what's wrong, choose to appreciate what's right.

Set boundaries. It's common for families to want to be involved in the details of each other's lives. Sometimes this is welcomed, and other times it becomes a distraction or challenge. Most (but not all) of the time, it's done with good intentions. If extended family or in-laws are overstepping their bounds (for example, trying to parent your kids in ways you don't agree with), you may need to set boundaries that protect your immediate family. Talk with your spouse and decide together what boundaries to put in place.

Forgive. It's likely that at some point, someone in your extended family will do or say something that upsets or bothers you or your spouse. Instead of being hurt and bitter, choose to let it go. Taking offense and becoming angry or antagonistic will only make matters worse. By turning to the Savior, you can find the strength to forgive and move past the hurt. By choosing to forgive, you'll experience a weight being lifted off your shoulders and a freedom to move forward in faith, unencumbered by the past.

Be willing to help. One of the wonderful things about family is that you're there to lift each other up and extend a helping hand. Your parents or your spouse's parents will probably need caretaking at some point. Your siblings may experience difficulties and need extra support. If you're willing to step in and serve your family when needed, then love will grow—and you'll receive aid in kind when you need it. Choose to draw your family together by loving and serving one another and by creating a support network that will strengthen everyone through the good and the hard times.

As you try these suggestions, you'll find that, just as Malachi taught, one of the best ways to build a strong marriage is to turn your heart to your family. The love between you and your spouse will be strengthened as you accept each other's families and allow yourself to love them just as they are.

FOR DISCUSSION

- What traditions, habits, and rituals do you each want to incorporate into your marriage from your respective families?

- What positive things did you see your parents do to strengthen their marriage? What did you see that you didn't like?

- What kind of family culture do you and your spouse want to create?

- Are there any unresolved experiences from your youth or childhood that make it difficult for you to turn your heart to your family? How can that be resolved?

- Whom do you need to forgive, serve, and love in order to strengthen your family ties?

- How has experiencing healing with your extended family or in-laws blessed your marriage?

learning to *love*

Thou shalt love the Lord thy God with all thy heart, and with all thy soul, and with all thy mind. This is the first and great commandment. And the second is like unto it, Thou shalt love thy neighbour as thyself.
Matthew 22:37–39

Before we were married, Aaron met with a church leader and mentor to talk about our upcoming marriage and the importance of the covenant he would be entering into. During the course of their conversation, they spoke of priorities, devotion to God, and the love that April and Aaron had for each other. In that meeting, he was reminded that perhaps one of the best ways we could learn to love the Lord as He has invited us to do would be to truly learn to love each other with a Christlike love.

That lesson has stayed with Aaron through all these years, and he has often pondered his love and commitment to God and to April, and how that love manifests in both inward and outward ways. It seems to be one of the great quests of life: to exhibit a deep and devoted love for God, spouse, and family, and to consistently show that love through thought, word, and deed. Saying "I love you" is easy enough, but showing it consistently is a whole different story.

We cannot fully love God without loving our spouses, and we cannot love our spouses fully without loving God. God's ways are perfect, and He has established a plan whereby we can learn and grow by experiencing opportunities that stretch us and help us learn to love others, as imperfect as each of us may be.

Showing your love for the Lord by genuinely loving your spouse is a perfect application of this week's scripture. Your love for God should strengthen your love for your spouse, and your love for your spouse will strengthen your love for God. This interaction creates an upward spiral effect, leading to a greater unity in your marriage and a closer connection with God. As your love for God grows, you'll feel a natural inclination to express that love through kindness and service to those closest to you. As your love for your spouse grows, you'll feel a natural inclination to thank God for the blessing of your spouse in your life.

There will be times when you may not feel a lot of love for your spouse. Try not to get discouraged, and never give up. Love is a choice, a commitment, a gift. You aren't expected to be perfect. You're simply expected to make your very best effort and keep moving forward. So be patient with yourself.

God invites us to love not because He *needs* our love but because He *is* love. By learning to love as He does, we'll come to know Him better and experience the joy and life that He knows.

FOR DISCUSSION

- How can your love for God become a driving influence for how you treat your spouse?

- What does true love for God look like? How is it reflected in your daily actions toward others?

- How is your love for God changing the way you relate to your spouse?

- What will happen in your marriage when you love your spouse with all your heart?

FURTHER READING

- Romans 8:38–39
- Matthew 25:40
- Ephesians 5:33

treasures in *heaven*

> Lay not up for yourselves treasures upon earth. . . . But lay up for yourselves treasures in heaven, where neither moth nor rust doth corrupt, and where thieves do not break through nor steal: For where your treasure is, there will your heart be also.
> Matthew 6:19–21

In marriage, you have to constantly evaluate your priorities, your desires, and the treasures you're seeking so that you don't fall off the track you really want to be on. While there's nothing inherently wrong with worldly success—in fact, we ought to push ourselves and work hard to become all that we can become—the sole pursuit of materialism and power at any expense necessary is not healthy. If left unchecked, it can blind you from eternal priorities and cause problems in your marriage.

Why? When our desires are focused on gaining approval from the world, we miss the mark. We forget what matters most and too easily neglect the God-given opportunities and responsibilities that are intended to help us grow and experience lasting joy. For example, consider each of the following "treasures," all of which may be important and necessary to a certain degree but which definitely aren't worth sacrificing your treasures in heaven.

Career. Success in one's career can be a great blessing—some of the people we admire most have enjoyed great success in their chosen vocations. But that success doesn't define them. There are plenty of stories about individuals who spend their lives climbing the career ladder, only to find when they reach the top that the ladder was leaning against the wrong wall all along. No professional success is worth sacrificing your greatest treasured relationships. What's the point of excelling in your career if you leave behind a broken marriage and shattered relationships with your children? Be careful and intentional regarding the trade-offs you are willing to make for work. It would be wise for both of you to evaluate your careers from time to time. Discuss aspects of your jobs that are blessing your marriage and family and those that aren't. Pray for the right opportunities and for inspiration about the knowledge, skills, and connections you need now in order to be able to do more good later.

Money. Far too many people spend the majority of their lives chasing the elusive dollar, only to learn that the road it leads down can be cruel, cold, and lonely. Can money resolve some of life's challenges? Of course. Can money provide some of the frills, thrills, and comforts we all enjoy from time to time? Naturally. But money alone will not make you happy or bring you lasting joy. There's nothing wrong with striving for success or acquiring personal wealth—it's something we all seek. But carefully guard those pursuits against an all-encompassing drive for wealth that could consume your best efforts and leave little behind for those you love most.

Personal image and "keeping up." It's natural to look sideways to see what everyone else is doing. You may be feeling pressure to drive a certain car, own a certain home, or acquire certain things just because someone down the street does. Enjoying some earthly trappings is not wrong in and of itself, but if you're doing these things simply to keep up a certain appearance or feel good about yourself, beware (especially if those trappings are funded by consumer debt)! That kind of motivation can easily lead to conflict and strain and can overtake the health of any marriage and family. Rather than yielding to outside voices pressuring you to look, act, and be a certain way, determine what your priorities are and stick to them. Be comfortable in your own skin, and don't let fleeting trends or social media dictate how you live or spend your resources.

Now compare those to the eternal promises God makes to us—namely, treasures in heaven. While there are many treasures to be had in the world, they are just that—worldly and, therefore, temporary. The Savior invites us to focus our hearts on more heavenly things. Treasures in heaven are the things that last: knowledge, truth, and eternal relationships (like your relationship with your spouse). God will bless you to know which treasures to seek and which to let go of. While there's nothing inherently wrong with the pursuit of the things listed, they should not be "treasured" at the expense of a higher and more heavenly purpose.

As you commit to pursuing things of lasting value and laying up treasures in heaven, you'll find that your life becomes simpler, your purpose becomes clearer, and your joy increases. Your marriage will thrive as you keep it a top priority and seek God's approval instead of the world's. As you do that, God will be able to use you to accomplish His purposes, which have eternal and lasting value.

FOR DISCUSSION

- What are you currently pursuing that feels empty, unnecessarily complicated, or unhealthy for your marriage?

- What are your highest priorities, and do your actions accurately reflect them?

- Which earthly treasures (those listed earlier in the devotion or others) are a source of contention in your marriage? Why?

- What will you have to give up in order to pursue heavenly treasures?

- How will prayerfully pursuing heavenly treasures invite greater direction and purpose into your marriage and life?

I can do all things through *Christ* which strengtheneth me.

PHILIPPIANS 4:13

be *loyal* to each other

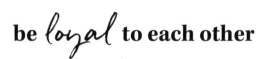

Ye have heard that it was said by them of old time,
Thou shalt not commit adultery: But I say unto you,
That whosoever looketh on a woman to lust after her
hath committed adultery with her already in his heart.
Matthew 5:27–28

The day you got married was the day you formally chose—and promised—to be committed and loyal to your spouse. On that day, you ended one season of life and started a new one.

But even after you've opened the door to this wonderful adventure called marriage, you must be careful to keep the romantic doors of your heart closed to anyone other than your spouse. Entertaining romantic thoughts or feelings for friends, coworkers, or other acquaintances will only damage the foundation of your marriage. For your marriage to thrive and blossom into everything it can become, you have to be fully committed to your one and only. Isn't it interesting that two of the Ten Commandments mention adultery or seeking someone other than your spouse? Those directives exist to keep you and your relationship safe and on track.

Let's be very real and honest here. Even after you're married, you're going to find other people attractive in physical, emotional, intellectual, or even spiritual ways. That is normal. It's what you think, say, or do *after* noticing that attraction that will make all the difference in who you become, how happy you are, and the kind of marriage you enjoy.

If an attractive coworker invites you over for dinner, or sends you lots of text messages after hours, or wants to hang out on the weekend, it can be easy to justify it as building a better working relationship. It can be flattering or exciting to have a pretty girl flirt with you at the gym or to have an intelligent man listen intently to your emotional needs—particularly if you're missing that kind of connection with your spouse.

Each of these situations may seem harmless at first, and as isolated events they probably are. The problem is that these small occurrences compound over time, and the door to your heart and mind may open more and more to someone other than your spouse. Once that door is open even a little, it can be difficult to discern how far you've gone and to turn back. Remember that just as doors swing on very small hinges, small thoughts or acts can lead to large consequences.

In order to be loyal to your spouse, you have to resist temptation. The Adversary is a master tempter, and he is forever trying to distract you from what matters most: a happy marriage and family. Temptation will come, but every temptation is simply a choice—a door that is opened to you that you have the power to quickly close. One of the best ways to keep the doors of your heart and mind from swinging open is to take care of your marriage. When your needs aren't being met, you're in more danger of turning to someone else to meet those needs.

With the Savior's grace, it is absolutely possible to be true and loyal to your spouse in every way. This doesn't mean you'll never make mistakes, but it does mean you can pray and work for the strength, courage, and character to keep improving, overcoming, and closing doors.

As you and your spouse keep the doors of your hearts open only to each other, you'll be insulated from painful consequences and free to enjoy the fulfillment and happiness that married life is intended to bring.

FOR DISCUSSION

- What kind of attention and love do you and your spouse need from each other?

- Write down one thing you can do for your spouse to better meet his/her needs.

- Read Ephesians 6:10–18 together. What stands out to you from this passage? Why is it important to put on the whole armor of God? How can this help you keep the promises you made on your wedding day to be loyal to each other?

deliverance from
addiction and affliction

> Our soul is escaped as a bird out of the snare of the fowlers:
> the snare is broken, and we are escaped.
> Psalm 124:7

Aaron's dad was raised on a ranch, and, as a result, Aaron grew up hearing story after story about ranch life. Some of his favorites were about hunting and trapping. His dad would explain how he'd carefully set traps in hopes of catching a predator before it could hurt their sheep. If done properly, the predator would be lured in close, tempted by a scent or piece of meat, and then caught by a cleverly hidden trap.

Addictions are some of Satan's most powerful traps that he sets to ensnare us. These traps can keep us from experiencing the joy and fulfillment that God wants for each of His children. His plan is for us to be free to choose—but when individuals are caught in the trap of addiction, the gift of choice is often hampered by clouded judgment.

As with other illnesses or diseases, healing from an addiction often requires help from a trained professional. If you are dealing with an addiction, we encourage you—and your families and loved ones—to seek aid from professionals and support networks who can help you overcome this challenge. As you do so, remember to turn to the Master Healer, Jesus Christ, who loves you and who can help buoy you up during your deepest and darkest hours. His power to help and heal is real and available to you.

One of the best ways to prevent addiction is to stay close to God and avoid the temptation before it even shows up. As Lynn G. Robbins once said, "It is easier to avoid temptation than it is to resist temptation." To prevent the painful effects of addiction from creeping into your life, stay close to God and to your spouse. Fill your life with healthy habits that bring you joy, and surround yourself with people who lift you up and make you better. Addictions often grow out of an unmet need for connection or as a way of numbing pain, loneliness, anxiety, or any other negative emotion. When you stay close to God and good friends, the power of temptation is greatly diminished.

If your spouse is caught in a destructive cycle of addiction, know that you don't need to, nor should you, bear that burden alone. Reach out to trusted family or friends who can provide support. Encourage your spouse to seek professional help, and take advantage of those resources for yourself as well. Seek heaven's help by spending more time in the scriptures and in prayer. As you do this, you'll come to know God better and feel His love for you. Please know that your spouse's addiction is not your fault, and it's not your responsibility to fix it.

The New Testament contains a powerful story of the Savior providing long-awaited healing. In Matthew 9, we read about a woman who "was diseased with an issue of blood." Despite seeing many doctors and suffering from this ailment for 12 years, she was unable to find the healing she needed and wanted. In utter desperation, she turned to the Savior. She had faith that if she could just touch the hem of His clothing, she would be healed. And so, she sought Christ, reached out, and simply touched Him. Jesus, feeling that virtue had "gone out of" Him (Luke 8:46), turned around and spoke peace and encouragement to the woman.

He told her, "Daughter, be of good comfort; thy faith hath made thee whole" (Matthew 9:22).

She was healed.

In your desperation, we invite you to reach out to Jesus Christ, trusting that He will heal you, too. He can strengthen you against temptation, help you control your cravings, and give you strength and courage to consistently choose a life of freedom and protection.

FOR DISCUSSION

- How are you protecting against addiction individually and as a couple?
- How can taking care of your physical and spiritual health protect you against addiction or help you navigate out of it?
- If you struggle with addiction, what is the next step you can take in turning toward the Savior and accessing His help?
- What professional resources can you tap into that can help in overcoming addiction?

FURTHER READING

- Read John 5:1–9. What similarities can you draw from this story to your own life? How does the Savior's question to the man with the infirmity in verse 6 make you feel?
- Read Galatians 6:2. What can spouses do to encourage and strengthen each other during addiction recovery?
- Read 2 Chronicles 30:8–9. How will turning to the Lord help your spouse find compassion before "them that lead them captive"? What will this mean in your daily life?
- Read Psalm 107:6–9. How will knowing that God can satisfy the very longings of your soul help you turn to Him instead of your addiction?

prayerfully making decisions *together*

In every thing by prayer and supplication with thanksgiving let your requests be made known unto God.
Philippians 4:6

We recently had to make a big decision about a job opportunity that would take our young family across the country. We struggled with the decision and grappled through all the pros and cons for our careers, finances, family, marriage, homelife, and future. We prayed, talked, and sought advice from family and friends. Finally, we decided to accept the offer. The transition would be fast, and we would move in less than three weeks, so we immediately began packing up the house and working out the details of the move.

But then, a few days later, we woke up feeling very uneasy about our decision. From prior experience, we had learned that the uneasy feeling could mean one of two things: (1) we had a big change coming and we were overwhelmed and nervous, or (2) God wanted something different for us at that time. We again went through the process of being prayerful and counseling together, and ultimately, we realized that we needed to course-correct. God had given us a chance to make a decision and learn for ourselves that this was not the best path for us.

Sometimes, when you're faced with two options, you have to travel down the wrong path for a short while so you can know with surety what the right path is. It took courage, faith, and a lot of nerve to turn down the job offer, but it was the right decision. Going through the process of prayerfully making this decision together drew us closer to each other and to God.

There are so many decisions to make in marriage. How will you successfully navigate the myriad choices you encounter at each stage of your lives? What will you do when faced with a challenge that requires difficult decisions to be made? How will you come to an agreement about what is best for your marriage and family?

God wants to be involved in your decisions. He doesn't want to make your decisions for you, but He wants to help you learn how to make really good ones. He freely allows you to choose which path to take so you can learn to exercise your agency to create the best life possible. At the same time, He also wants you to seek His guidance and do His will. He watches over your life and has a plan for you. If you learn to listen with your heart, you will know whether or not the choices you're making are in line with His will for you.

Here are four suggestions that may help you prayerfully make big decisions together:

1. **Remember that marriage is an equal partnership.** Don't make big life decisions alone. Although some decisions may seem focused on one spouse more than the other, once you're married, every decision affects you both as a couple. Remember that you each have a voice and that one of the beauties of marriage is in coming together and finding unity. So respect and value each other's opinions, perspectives, and feelings, and have confidence that you can successfully make decisions together.

2. **Spend time counseling together.** New ideas will come as you counsel together and talk through your thoughts, feelings, and concerns. This pattern and process, when done prayerfully, invites the Spirit to guide your minds and hearts and to help you both come to a unity about what's best for *your* situation. Evaluate your priorities and values, and remember that there often has to be give and take from both individuals in order to reach a decision you both feel good about.

3. **Pray about the decision.** God wants you to learn the pattern of decision-making. That pattern typically starts with studying the problem yourself, doing your homework, and reaching your own conclusion. Then, take your conclusion to God in prayer and seek His counsel. As you pray, carefully listen for His direction. Answers can come in many

ways but often become clear when we take the time to be still, search the scriptures, and pay attention to the thoughts and feelings that come to us. When we follow this pattern, we may feel confident about what we've decided, or feel uneasy about it, or feel that God simply trusts us to make this decision ourselves. We use our best reasoning and judgment, and we listen to our hearts.

4. **Move forward in faith.** Sometimes, confirmation that you've made the right decision doesn't come until you begin to act on that decision. As you exercise your faith through action, God can reaffirm your choice, correct and warn you, or guide you down a slightly different but better path that only He can see. Just remember, you can't do better than the Lord's will for you.

If you're not facing any big decisions together right now, pray about what your next step might be. God will direct your path and offer you opportunities for living the purposeful life that you both want to live.

FOR DISCUSSION

- Take turns sharing a big decision that has been weighing on your minds. What is one specific thing you can do to help each other through this process of making a decision and moving forward in faith?
- How has God helped you make decisions in the past? What have you learned from your experiences so far? How has your confidence in God grown through these experiences?

CHALLENGE

Write down three decisions you need to make this month. Then take them to the Lord in prayer and practice the pattern mentioned in the discussion points.

lessons in *courage*

Have I not commanded thee? Be strong and of a good courage; be not afraid, neither be thou dismayed: for the Lord thy God is with thee whithersoever thou goest.
Joshua 1:9

It isn't always easy to keep the promises you made on your wedding day. Sometimes it's difficult to endure, to be committed, and to work through difficult seasons or growing pains. You'll need courage to face these trials with faith, to be loyal to God and your spouse through the hard times, and to see the good things the future holds for you. Remember that whatever your situation is, in Christ you can receive the courage to press forward with faith and have confidence in your future.

Queen Esther's story, found in the book of Esther, is certainly one of being courageous with a spouse. She faced a difficult situation when she found out that a wicked advisor had convinced her husband, the king of Persia, to issue a royal decree stating that every Jew would be killed. Unbeknownst to the king, Esther herself was a Jew, which placed her in a situation that would have tried any individual. She could remain quiet and enjoy her life of luxury and privilege, hoping her nationality would never be discovered, or she could put her own life at risk and speak out on behalf of her family, her friends, and all of the Jews in the kingdom.

It must have been hard to face such a stressful and threatening situation. Esther could have chosen fear, worry, and blame. But her uncle Mordecai reminded her that God's hand was in all this and that it was possibly for this very reason that she had been chosen to be the queen at this time. And so, she chose to have courage. She chose to have faith. She chose to go to the king and defend her people, even though her very life was at stake.

Because she faced this difficult choice with conviction and trust in God, a miracle occurred. She explained to the king his advisor's plot to kill the Jews and pleaded with him to rescind the law. She was able to convince the king to issue a second decree, stating that the Jews could arm and defend themselves and their property. Her life and the lives of her people were preserved, and God blessed Esther because of her courage.

You will have hard choices to make in the coming days, months, and years. Like Esther, you will need to be brave if you're to make the right choice no matter what situation you face. It will take courage to bring up tough but important issues with your spouse that neither of you are comfortable talking about. It will take courage to express your feelings about what you need sexually from your spouse. It will take courage to admit you were wrong, ask for forgiveness, and patiently wait for healing, to raise kids, take care of aging parents, and remain faithful no matter what. But if God helped Esther talk to her spouse about matters of life and death, He will help you, too.

As it says in this week's scripture, God commands and invites you to be strong and to have courage—but He doesn't say you have to do it all on your own strength. He promises that He will be with you through all the ups and downs that married life will bring. You've got this! We're cheering for you.

FOR DISCUSSION

Read the following passages and be open with each other as you answer the accompanying questions.

- 1 Chronicles 28:20. What is something you're afraid of talking about, working on, or facing in your life or in your marriage?

- Psalm 27:1. How can coming to know God and spending time with Him fill you with courage? What do you desperately need courage to say, do, or change?

- Philippians 4:13. What is the heavenly help that is available to you? What does this help have to do with courage?

when feelings are *hurt*

He healeth the broken in heart, and bindeth up
their wounds.
Psalm 147:3

In our 10 years of marriage, we've shared a lot of beautiful times and a few less-than-beautiful times. In short, we've shared real life together. In the course of everyday living, we have sometimes hurt each other with things we've said, ways we've reacted to each other, or things we have or haven't done. Some of those hurts have been more painful than others, but we've learned that there is a very real way to overcome them.

It's all too easy and very normal to get your feelings hurt. When your spouse says something less than loving, your natural tendency, like ours, may be to feel upset. To feel sad. To start making a mental list of all the things your spouse is doing wrong and how thoughtless and hard to deal with they are. In these painful moments, you might give your spouse the silent treatment or even start an argument.

But when emotions run high and hurt runs deep and the tension between you is noticeable, that's when Satan is winning. He wants you to really dislike, even hate each other. He'll fill your mind with memories of all the times your spouse has failed you or been the wrong person for you, convincing you that you don't need to apologize and that you and your spouse can never be happy together. He'll tell you that your marriage is too far gone, that you'll always be fighting and hurting.

When you feel caught in the negative cycle of being hurt and wanting to stay hurt, you have a choice to make. You can choose to remain upset, or you can choose to take a step back, pray, and let the Savior help you navigate your emotions and true desires. When you turn to the Savior,

He will grant you the strength to make the choices that are necessary to let the hurt go. These choices include the following:

Choose healing. When you get on your knees and seek heaven's help for your marriage, you're choosing healing. You're choosing to walk down the road toward help and happiness. It's one of the very best choices you could ever make in your marriage.

Choose love. You may not be feeling much love for your spouse right now, but if you pray for it and work for it, love will come. If you choose to *act* like you love your spouse, even if you don't feel it, then love will start to grow again. Perhaps the very best way to choose love in marriage is to choose to see your spouse for who they are and can *become*, no matter what your spouse has said or done.

Choose to apologize. Often, when you're hurt, pride runs deep, and you don't even want to entertain thoughts about apologizing. However, if you can muster enough humility and courage to simply apologize for the way you acted or for what you said in anger or bitterness, you can begin the healing process and invite the Savior to rebuild your marriage. In our experience, it only takes one of us being humble enough to apologize to quickly dispel the hurt we've been feeling and to immediately restore peace, love, and joy to our marriage.

Choose to forgive. Only the Savior can heal your heart and your hurt. He can help you forgive, freeing you from the burden and pain of bitterness. No matter how long the hurt has been festering or how deep the pain goes, forgiveness is a gift you can receive from Him this very hour, if you so choose. It is perhaps the most sacred and meaningful gift that you can offer your spouse as well. We must note here: If you're suffering abuse of any kind, seek help immediately.

If you choose to let the Savior in, He will bind up your wounds and offer you the miracle of a marriage restored in and through Him.

FOR DISCUSSION

Read Psalm 34:18, Psalm 73:26, and Revelation 21:4, and share your feelings with each other about the Savior and what He can do for your marriage.

- What do you feel inspired to choose to do because of what you have read?

- Which of the four choices mentioned do you most feel you need to make?

- What miracles could take place in your marriage if you let go of the hurts you're still holding on to?

- How have you experienced the healing power of the Savior in the past, and how can remembering these sacred moments help you in your current situation?

CHALLENGE

On separate pieces of paper, write down all of the hurts that are eating away at your soul. Then go and rip those papers up, throw them in the garbage, and decide once and for all to let the Savior help you let those things go. Obviously, a simple exercise like this won't fix everything, but it will remind you that you are, in this moment, making a choice to begin the restoration process that is available in and through Jesus Christ.

your way isn't always the *right* way

Jesus saith unto him, I am the way, the truth, and the life: no man cometh unto the Father, but by me.
John 14:6

By nature, humans can be stubborn creatures. This quality is particularly evident in marriage when two unique individuals try to combine their unique ways of doing things into the same household—and stay happy while doing it. When someone has a different approach than what we're used to, it can seem foreign, weird, and even a little annoying. For example, one of you may prefer to spend Saturday mornings in bed while the other wants to get up early. One of you may be a spender while the other might want to save every penny. We all have our own ways.

As a result, even subtle differences can quickly magnify and compound into unspoken frustrations. When those frustrations are voiced, couples can find themselves in a tough spot: Both individuals feel they're right, and neither is willing to change.

We tend to see things from one perspective: our own. And we usually think we are right. It takes a lot of humility to recognize that there may be better—or simply different—ways of doing things. But developing that ability will pay huge dividends in your marriage. Seeking a better understanding of your spouse's background and perspective can make you more patient, flexible, and accepting about the way he/she does things.

"The times that I am happiest and most fulfilled in my marriage are the times when I am intent on drawing meaning and fulfillment from becoming a better husband rather than from demanding a 'better' wife."
—Gary Thomas

While we each have our individual ways of being and doing, it's important to not let those little things become big sources of contention. Why would you let preferences over paper versus plastic or a little mess in the bathroom sink become a wedge between you and your spouse? In the grand scheme of things, those issues just don't matter, and we should keep them in proper perspective in our marriages. What we need to seek is alignment on the things that really do matter—the big things. And the alignment we're seeking is not with "my way" or "your way" but with God's way.

Consider the verse that begins this devotion. Ultimately, Jesus Christ is the way, and we should seek to align our will with His, just like He aligned His will with His Father's. You see, your way (or your spouse's way) may or may not be the *right* way, but His way always is. He said, "For I have given you an example, that ye should do as I have done to you. . . . If ye know these things, happy are ye if ye do them" (John 13:15, 17). Jesus is the way to happiness and peace in marriage. He is the way to change and progress in marriage. He knows what works and what will bring true success. Trust Him.

FOR DISCUSSION

- In what specific areas is *your* way not producing the results you hoped for in your marriage?

- How do you currently respond when you both think your way is the right way?

- What would it take to recognize that the Savior provides a better way?

- Read Isaiah 55:8–9 together. What do you notice about the differences between God's ways and your ways? How does understanding this change the way you feel about God's ways? How will this change your life this week?

- Study Matthew 5 together and take particular note of the phrase, "ye have heard that it was said by them of old time," and then make a list of the old ways the Savior replaced with new ones. Study these new ways and search your heart. How can you replace one of your old ways with a new way this week?

connected *conversations*

> And they talked together of all these things which had happened. And it came to pass, that, while they communed together and reasoned, Jesus himself drew near, and went with them.
> Luke 24:14–15

We were recently approached by a sincere wife who asked if it was possible for a couple, after years of challenge, to develop healthy communication habits. We responded with a resounding yes! Why? Because couples *can* learn and progress together, regardless of their current state. If they're willing to soften their hearts, work hard, and seek help, they can learn to share normal and beautiful conversations that will bring them closer together, strengthen their connection, and nurture their marriage.

Here are four simple, practical tips to help you start talking more and communicating better about the things that really matter.

1. **Acknowledge each other.** When you wake up, go to sleep, leave, come home, or walk into a room, acknowledge your spouse with words—even just a simple "hey, babe" or "you look nice." By acknowledging your spouse's presence in a friendly and engaging manner, you'll help conversation flow more naturally.

2. **Share first.** If you and your spouse have a hard time talking, decide to be the one who will share first. Share the details of your day, even the seemingly normal ones. What was funny, what was hard, and what do you need advice on? Practice your storytelling skills. As you open up to your spouse about your day, he or she will be more likely to open up to you as well.

3. **Open your heart.** At some point, if you really want to feel close to your spouse and be madly in love again, you'll need to be willing

to share more than surface-level feelings. Share your emotions, your goals, and your dreams. This may not come naturally to some people, but it is something you can get better at and more comfortable with through practice. As you learn to be vulnerable, real, and sensitive, good things will happen.

4. **Ask meaningful questions.** Avoid yes-or-no questions, and if your spouse gives you a one-word answer, try to ask a follow-up question. Ask about your spouse's worries, fears, hobbies, interests, and favorite pastimes. Actively listen to what your spouse shares with you and validate their thoughts, feelings, and opinions.

As you practice these simple tips, try incorporating a few rituals and routines into your marriage to help you become more intentional about connected conversations. Routines can strengthen and bless couples because they bring stability, meaning, and consistency to marriage. Here are a few suggestions that may help you and your spouse communicate better and more often.

Touch base daily. Stay in contact with your spouse throughout the day by texting, calling during lunch, or sending a quick e-mail. These simple, short connections offer the opportunity to flirt a little, compliment, thank, or simply keep each other in the loop.

Couch talk. If possible, intentionally carve out 10 minutes a day to sit with each other on the couch, without the distraction of technology, children, or food, just to catch up. If you feel like you don't have much to say, that's okay. Just share that moment together.

Pillow talk. Take time to talk when you're in bed together at night. There is something calming about bedtime that creates a safe place to share your thoughts with each other.

Walk and talk. Find a way to get outside, move your body, and talk. You may want to ride bikes together or walk around a park. As you take the time to do something healthy, energizing, and renewing together, you'll invite natural conversation and help your friendship grow.

Drive and talk. If you're like us, you'll find that some of your best conversations happen on long drives together. Take advantage of that shared time in a relatively confined space.

Long-distance talk. If one of you is out of town, make a commitment to call or video chat with each other. Those meaningful connections from a long distance can send a powerful message and can keep your marriage strong.

Couple councils. One healthy way to improve your communication is to set aside regular time for a couple's meeting. These meetings, or "councils," are an opportunity to do exactly what the name suggests: *counsel* with each other. Share what's going on, schedule your upcoming week, express appreciation for each other, and discuss ways you can help and support one another. Celebrate what's going well in your relationship, and plan ways to improve. Be open and humble, sharing anything you may be having a hard time with, personally or in the relationship. These councils can be eye-opening experiences that greatly improve the quality of your relationship.

As you sincerely implement any of these rituals into your marriage, you'll notice a difference. You'll pay more attention to each other; take note of the stressors, joys, and challenges you each face; and find better ways to lift, serve, and encourage each other. You'll feel closer, more connected, and more in love than you've felt in a long time.

FOR DISCUSSION

- What can you do to help each other feel safe and comfortable talking about what's in your heart?

- What lessons do you learn from this week's scripture passage about the importance of talking?

- Read Colossians 4:6. How can listening to the Spirit help you know how to respond to each other?

doing the work of *God*

For I have given you an example, that ye should do
as I have done to you. . . . If ye know these things,
happy are ye if ye do them.
John 13:15, 17

It was a sunny fall afternoon nine years ago. We had brought our first son, Michael, home from the hospital, and Aaron had left to get April something she needed. She sat on the couch in the living room, scriptures in hand, with the sun pouring in through the window. As she read Matthew 25, God taught her a beautiful lesson that would prove to be a great reminder to her throughout the upcoming years. He taught her that when she is caring for His children in even the most basic, ordinary, and prosaic ways, she is doing the work of God.

Matthew 25:31–46 contains the parable of the sheep and the goats, in which the Savior explains that those who will dwell with Him in His kingdom are those who have served Him: "For I was an hungred, and ye gave me meat: I was thirsty, and ye gave me drink: I was a stranger, and ye took me in: Naked, and ye clothed me: I was sick, and ye visited me: I was in prison, and ye came unto me." In the story, the righteous are confused and ask Him when they did these things for Him. The Savior responds by teaching this beautiful truth: "Verily I say unto you, Inasmuch as ye have done it unto one of the least of these my brethren, ye have done it unto me." Ministering to others in loving ways is one of the most obvious ways we can show our love for God and follow His example.

On the couch that fall day, the Spirit taught April that her new responsibilities of feeding, clothing, and caring for our newborn baby were an invitation to participate in His work and that these kinds of selfless acts would help qualify her to be found on His right hand in the hereafter. It was encouraging. He wasn't asking her to go out and change the world in some magnificent way. He was simply asking her to serve in her own capacity, beginning with our own family in our own home.

What she didn't know then was how very difficult and demanding it could be to serve and minister in a Christlike way to those you love the most. In all family relationships, including marriage, there are moments of frustration where you feel like you're making zero progress. There are moments of disappointment when you feel like you'll never succeed. But even when you experience those moments, don't give up. Keep pressing forward with courage and faith, knowing that you're doing the work of God. Doing the work of God won't always be easy, but it will most certainly be worth it.

Each day you have the opportunity to do God's work within the walls of your own home. It might not always be glamorous. It may sometimes even feel thankless. But it will never go unnoticed by God. When you're doing His work, you'll have His Spirit, and when you have His Spirit, you'll be filled with His love. This love will strengthen, even transform your relationship with your spouse. As you serve selflessly and do the everyday but essential work of God—feeding, clothing, caring for, providing, encouraging, listening, comforting, and supporting—within the walls of your home, you'll find greater purpose, joy, and satisfaction in your marriage, and you'll come to understand more fully the lesson the Savior taught that when you serve others, you're also serving Him.

FOR DISCUSSION

○ How have you benefited from your spouse's selfless service?

○ What is keeping you from meeting your spouse's needs?

○ Why is selfless service one of the great keys to a happy marriage?

○ Read Galatians 6:9–10 and Acts 10:38. What does it look like to "go about doing good" in your marriage and family? How do these passages apply to your marriage?

CHALLENGE

Write down seven ways you can minister to your spouse this week. Perform one of these acts of service each day for a week.

work on yourself *first*

> How wilt thou say to thy brother, Let me pull out the mote out of thine eye; and, behold, a beam is in thine own eye? Thou hypocrite, first cast out the beam out of thine own eye; and then shalt thou see clearly to cast out the mote out of thy brother's eye.
>
> Matthew 7:4–5

The Savior often used parables to teach His disciples eternal lessons. In the verse of this devotion, a "mote" is something small, like a speck of dust, while a beam is something quite large, like a wooden plank. In brief, we too often see other people's faults but don't recognize our own.

It may not be fun or comfortable to apply this parable to your marriage, but it's critically important if you're to have the kind of relationship you want. It's easy to become so consumed with fixing what you see as your spouse's problems that you neglect the things *you* need to work on in order to improve your marriage. Recognizing your own faults requires you to look inward, intentionally acknowledge where you're in the wrong, and be humble enough to work toward positive change.

There are certain things people sometimes say when they see a mote in their spouse's eye. For this activity, place a check next to any "mote phrases" that sound familiar to you or that you may have used in the past. Discuss how it makes you feel when you hear your spouse say one.

☐ "You need to change _____."

☐ "Stop doing _____."

☐ "Why do you always _____?"

☐ "I hate when you _____."

☐ "You never _____!"

☐ "When will you learn?"

☐ "You have issues."

☐ "I didn't do anything wrong."

☐ "It's your fault."

☐ "Why can't you see that you're the problem here?"

☐ "Do you hear yourself right now?"

Now, let's review some phrases that can help you take more responsibility for your own actions. These phrases can help you look inward, be humble, and decide on steps you can take to work toward inner change, resulting in a happier marriage.

Check the "beam phrases" that you would love to say to or hear from your spouse. Share your thoughts and feelings on these phrases with each other, and in your journal, write a few more that would be helpful in your relationship.

☐ "I see that by saying that, I hurt your feelings. I'm sorry."

☐ "I didn't realize until now that when I responded that way, you felt unloved."

☐ "I'm sorry it's taken me so long to see how proud and hotheaded I've been about this particular issue."

☐ "I see why you feel that way."

☐ "I often feel like _____ when you respond in _____ way."

☐ "The way I see things is _____, but I recognize that may not be how you see things."

☐ "Can you help me understand this from your perspective?"

☐ "I'm really working on this, and I promise I'll do better. I'll start by doing _____."

☐ "Will you share your heart with me? What bothers you most about _____?"

☐ "I can clearly see that when I did/said _____, it contributed to _____."

☐ "Can you help me understand how I could approach this situation better next time?"

☐ "What am I currently doing that is hurting or frustrating you?"

☐ "Are there things I say that make you feel unloved or disrespected?"

As you begin this journey, pray for the ability to see your spouse as they truly are and to recognize the specific steps you can take toward improvement. As you begin to see your spouse more clearly, your heart will soften, attacks and criticism will cease, and a Christlike love will bring healing and harmony into your marriage. That's a goal worth working toward, no matter how uncomfortable it might be in the short term.

FOR DISCUSSION

- In what ways do these phrases harm/help marital relationships?
- What is the true need the person using these phrases is trying to express?
- How does taking responsibility and looking inward change how couples can successfully navigate through difficult moments together?
- Why is taking responsibility for personal change so important in a marriage?
- How will looking inward and working on yourself help bring about more harmony in your relationship?
- What will happen when you work on your personal habits and improving yourself first, instead of wishing your spouse would change?

knowing your spouse

And Adam knew Eve his wife; and she conceived.
Genesis 4:1

In this week's scripture, we read that after they were cast out of Eden, Adam "knew" Eve, and they had a child. In ancient Hebrew, the word for "know," as in "have knowledge of," was also used to mean "have sexual intercourse with."

Couples who truly know each other in the fullest sense of the word are familiar with each other in both ways. They have knowledge of each other, spending time together, sharing their thoughts and feelings, perceiving each other's likes and dislikes, and finding ways to serve each other. They're well acquainted with each other's strengths and weaknesses, as well as each other's hopes, needs, and challenges. And they also express love and physical affection on a regular basis, including prioritizing sexual intimacy.

When couples grow apart, it's often because they simply stop doing things that help them really know each other. They stop spending time together, having fun together, and sharing intimate moments together. If this sounds a little like you and your spouse, and you're worried that you don't really know your spouse anymore, then take heart. It only takes a few intentional changes to rekindle that flame of connection, unity, and love you once felt for each other.

Here are some practical ways to nurture intimacy in your marriage in order to help you know each other again.

NURTURE YOUR FRIENDSHIP

This may sound overly simplistic, but in order to nurture friendship, you need to do the things that friends do. Talk, listen, laugh, and spend time together. Text, call, and communicate with each other every day. Remember little things the other person likes. Be there for each other. Plan romantic getaways and rekindle the romance you once knew and lived for. Novelty invites romance, so be adventurous and try new things together. Read books, take classes, and explore new hobbies. Try things your spouse loves, even if they don't sound very exciting to you at first; making an effort to at least appreciate those things sends a clear message of genuine friendship.

The more time you spend getting to know your spouse better, the quicker love and romance will grow again. As you strengthen your friendship, other areas of intimacy will quickly fall into place.

STRENGTHEN YOUR EMOTIONAL CONNECTION

Be intentional about having meaningful conversations regularly. Get beyond the surface level, and enjoy a good heart-to-heart conversation. Express empathy and understanding when your spouse opens their heart to you, and be willing to share your own feelings and thoughts in return. Be sensitive, flexible, and patient as you learn to connect with your spouse emotionally.

Make sure to include more physical affection in the course of your day as well. Hold her hand in public, lean over and kiss him while you watch a show, cuddle with each other. The more tender physical affection in your relationship, the stronger your emotional connection will be.

Sharing your hearts with each other and intentionally offering physical affection throughout the day will lead you to develop a stronger emotional connection.

MAKE SEX A PRIORITY

Sex is a beautiful, unifying experience that spouses should enjoy on a regular basis. It's a divinely appointed means of bringing children into the world and an equally important way for husbands and wives to fully express their love for each other. Sex is the crowning act of physical intimacy. When you're married, you give yourself to each other, and sex is perhaps the ultimate physical expression of that gift. Sex is also a great responsibility: Your spouse has placed significant trust in you. That trust should always be kept and never violated in any way.

Sex is one of the very best ways to keep couples close to each other's hearts and on each other's minds. Sex invites couples to both give and receive, to trust and be vulnerable, and to enter a sacred and safe intimate space together. Sex is one of the most beautiful ways to draw couples together when distance, time, misunderstanding, or pain has separated them.

If you and/or your spouse have been rejecting each other or simply avoiding this important part of marriage, we urge you to discuss together what you can do to make sex a healthy, safe, and regular part of your lives again.

By nurturing your friendship, strengthening your emotional connection, and making sex a priority, you'll come to know each other better in every sense of the word, and that will increase the kindness, caring, satisfaction, and fulfillment in your marriage.

FOR DISCUSSION

Answer the following questions on separate pieces of paper and then exchange papers with each other. Keep your spouse's paper, and find ways to serve and love your spouse better based on what they've written down.

GETTING-TO-KNOW-YOU ACTIVITY

1. What is your favorite store-bought treat?

2. What is your favorite homemade dinner?

3. If you could have three wishes, what would they be?

4. What chore do you hate doing most?

5. Do you prefer a phone call or a text?

6. What is one of the biggest stressors you currently face?

7. It's a three-day weekend. What are two things you want to do?

8. What do you miss the most from when we were dating?

9. If you were to enroll in a community college continuing education class, what class would you choose?

10. What is one thing on your bucket list?

11. What is the most encouraging thing someone has said to you?

12. Name three date ideas that sound fun to you.

13. Where do you want to go on your next trip?

14. How often would you prefer to have sex?

15. What do you need most from me right now?

16. What are three things that make you feel loved?

when you have unmet *needs*

And God is able to make all grace abound toward you;
that ye, always having all sufficiency in all things, may
abound to every good work.
2 Corinthians 9:8

Recently, after a long day, we climbed into bed, exhausted. April wished Aaron would snuggle up to her and ask her how she was doing. But he just lay there—he'd had a long day, too, and in his mind, it was time for sleep. April thought, *Does he even care? Can't he tell that I need him?* But Aaron isn't a mind reader and didn't know what April wished he would do. So we did what two tired people normally do. We shared a goodnight peck, said, "I love you," and rolled over, not even touching.

If you've been married for any length of time, this situation likely feels familiar. We often feel our needs aren't being met and wonder why our spouses aren't acting the way we want them to. You may have had some of the following thoughts:

- He never wants to make any decisions; he just expects me to do it.
- I feel like she rules the roost and treats me like I'm her child.
- I'm lonely. We have nothing to talk about anymore.
- Why doesn't she greet me with a hug when she comes home instead of just complaining about her day?
- Did he notice everything I did today?
- He spends too much money.
- We always argue about the same things.
- She only wants to talk about the kids.
- Why doesn't he pay more attention to the kids?
- She never wants to have sex.

- He wants to have sex all the time.
- She never leaves me little notes anymore.
- He never brings me flowers.

As April lay in bed that night, God reminded her of a truth she needed to remember if we were to make it through the inevitable ups and downs of this beautiful thing called marriage: Aaron had needs, too (like getting some rest), and perhaps she wasn't doing as well as she thought at meeting those needs. In that moment, she was grateful that God helped her realize how easy it is be selfish in marriage. She thanked God for reminding her of how her thoughts and actions could quickly improve the quality of our marriage. She knew she had work to do and that God would help her do it.

There will be times when your spouse will not meet all your needs. Some spouses may be good at giving physical affection but lack the ability or desire to share intellectual intimacy. Or a spouse may be able to connect emotionally but lack the common know-how for buying gifts or planning dates. Sometimes your spouse is trying their best, but they may not know what your needs are or how to meet them. Instead of focusing on what your spouse isn't doing or providing for you, turn things around and see what you can do to better meet your spouse's needs.

It is also important to remember that when your spouse doesn't meet your needs, God can. Remember Philippians 4:19: "My God shall supply all your need." He can help you turn your thoughts from inward-focused to outward-focused, change your needs, strengthen you when your needs aren't being met, or help you forget your own needs by focusing on those of others.

Choosing to follow the example of Jesus Christ, to think truth-filled thoughts, and to change your behavior toward your spouse will invite the Savior's healing love to fill your heart. And by turning your thoughts and actions toward your spouse, you might actually invite the very connection, affection, and love that you seek. God knows the way to healing and happiness in marriage, so trust Him, move forward with faith, and never give up.

FOR DISCUSSION

- How can the Savior help me change my thought patterns and, therefore, my behavior?
- How can I give my spouse the time and attention they need from me?
- Do I respond to my spouse's invitations to participate more fully in the relationship? Am I all in when it comes to my marriage?
- How will doing something to meet my spouse's needs invite healing into our relationship?
- Together, read Philippians 2:5, 4:8, and 4:19. How do these pieces of scripture inform how you can change your thoughts and behaviors toward your spouse?

CHALLENGE

1. Write down the top three needs you have right now, and share your lists with each other.
2. Decide on one way you can try to meet one of those needs for your spouse this week, and then make it happen.
3. Start creating a list of all the things you love about your spouse. Add to this list any time negative thoughts about them come your way. Start training yourself to think positively by replacing negative thoughts about your spouse with positive ones.
4. Pray for your spouse. Pray to have positive thoughts about your spouse, to be less selfish, and to find ideas and resources that will help strengthen and protect your marriage.

resisting *pride*

> Be clothed with humility: for God resisteth the proud, and giveth grace to the humble. Humble yourselves therefore under the mighty hand of God, that he may exalt you in due time: Casting all your care upon him; for he careth for you.
> 1 Peter 5:5–7

It was late. We were tired and stressed, and a conflict had set us off. We should have gone to bed, but one of us prefers to talk things out and the other prefers to sleep on it. Naturally, pride got in the way, and we both tried to process this stressor in our own way. With emotions running high, April got the car keys and marched out the door to go for a drive.

Although she could feel God's Spirit whispering in her heart to calm down and not walk out that door, pride won. As she got in the car and started to back out of the driveway, all of the tears she'd been holding in came rushing out. So she began to do what she always does: pray. She prayed and cried, and a few hundred feet down the road, she made the decision to be humble, drive back home, and say she was sorry. The moment she decided to turn back, humility won, and she felt empowered and encouraged to love, apologize, and try again. As Aaron witnessed her response, those same feelings grew in his heart, too.

In this week's scripture, Peter teaches the truth that God gives grace to the humble. April felt the truth of those words on that discouraging night, the very moment she chose to be humble, to seek God's help in loving Aaron, and to look at herself and the changes she needed to make. Grace was a very real blessing that night. Humility won both of our hearts, and what could have been a much bigger argument ended up being something we both got over pretty quickly.

You may recognize pride when you act defensive, seek to control, think your way is the only right way, don't listen with your heart, or respond with impatience. Pride takes offense. Pride makes an angry exit. Pride stirs up conflict and invites emotions to spiral out of control. But God's miracle of grace is available if you humbly seek it. You will find, especially during difficult times, that grace can help you do what you cannot normally do on your own. It can help you recognize you have a choice, then help you choose to stay, move forward with hope, and surmount the obstacles that inevitably come to all who are married.

So the next time you find yourself in a conflict with your spouse, pause and ask yourself one simple question: "In this moment, will I choose to be proud or to be humble?" The choice is yours. We promise you that when you choose humility, heavenly help will come.

FOR DISCUSSION

Write. Take a few moments to write in your journals about times when you've chosen to be humble in your marriage. What did that look like, and how did you feel? How can you commit to consistently choosing humility over pride the next time conflict arises?

Share. When have you seen pride ruin the relationships of close family members or friends? What can you learn from their experiences, and how can you avoid making those same mistakes in your relationship?

Practice. The Dutch writer Corrie ten Boom wrote, "The will can function regardless of the temperature of the heart." How can you apply this concept to pride and humility in marriage? How will it change the way you act in your marriage this week?

CHALLENGE

Watch a movie or TV show together that showcases a marriage relationship (You may enjoy *Fireproof*, *Up*, or *Yours, Mine & Ours*). Afterward, analyze the way the couple interacted with each other. What did this couple do well? What made their relationship work? When did you see pride? When did you see humility? What did you like about how they treated each other or how they worked through conflict? What should they have done differently?

Let the *husband* render unto the wife due benevolence: and likewise also the *wife* unto the husband.

1 CORINTHIANS 7:3

be one

> For this cause shall a man leave his father and mother, and
> cleave to his wife; And they twain shall be one flesh: so then
> they are no more twain, but one flesh. What therefore God
> hath joined together, let not man put asunder.
> Mark 10:7–9

In the first three years of our marriage, there was a small thing that was
ever so gradually distancing us from each other. It was something we
didn't see eye to eye on, and so we both just kept doing what worked
best for us individually. We never really saw the need to talk about it or
figure out a way to change things. Neither of us had any creative solutions, and it seemed for a time that we were simply going to put up with
how things were.

Then, while on a trip together, we both felt ready to finally approach
this topic and find a solution. We both had humble hearts and were ready
to discuss something that up until this point had been too sensitive of
an issue to bring up. We both admitted that what we were doing wasn't
working. It took compromise, and it took trust, but together we arrived
at a new solution.

There was a palpable peace that accompanied our decision that day.
Moving forward would require a concerted effort, but we felt confident this
was the right thing for us to do. We became united about something we
had been divided on, and that simple decision has blessed our marriage for
over seven years now. We're so grateful for that unifying experience.

Every couple likely has an issue like this—finances, when and how
many children to have, parenting methods, religion, sexual intimacy,
work/career moves, friends, in-laws, or any number of other issues.
Differences of opinion are a natural and normal part of every marriage.
It's not possible to bring two unique people together and have every

routine, decision, and issue perfectly ironed out from day one. Some things simply take time, and that's okay. Rather than forcing the issue, it's often better to wait until both spouses are ready and unified in order to move forward hand in hand.

As you experience these opportunities to grow and be unified in decisions you make together, remember these three important principles:

1. **Show respect.** No matter your differences, if you choose to respect each other for who you are and what you bring to the table, you'll be able to work through just about anything. As you honor each other's values, perspectives, and opinions, you will learn from each other, find compromises that work, and come up with creative solutions that unify you as a couple.

2. **Communicate clearly.** Both spouses need to clearly communicate their perspectives and expectations in order to facilitate better compromise. If you listen humbly and share openly, you'll be prepared to think creatively, negotiate, and compromise until a united decision is achieved.

3. **Be patient.** In some cases, you'll achieve unity and make decisions rather quickly. In other cases, it will take time—sometimes lots of it. As you work on becoming more patient and humble, you'll be able to find solutions and see how two can become one.

As you seek to become one, you will quickly realize that you and your spouse are equal partners and that getting your way is not what's important. What's important is achieving harmony and moving forward together. There will be growing pains, but that's okay as long as you're moving in the right direction. It may take time, and it may not be possible on every issue, but the more you seek to achieve unity, the more the oneness you experience will fortify and bless your marriage, now and for years to come.

FOR DISCUSSION

- What is dividing you right now? What differences are keeping you from being unified?

- How will agreeing on the common values and goals you share help you understand each other better and make decisions in unity?

- How can being humble and sincerely listening to each other help you achieve unity?

- What would change if instead of saying "me," "my," and "I," you said "we," "us," and "ours"? What other phrases could you adjust in order to improve your unity?

- What one change can you make this week to help you two get on the same page and move forward as a team?

your money *stewardship*

> Wherefore do ye spend money for that which is not bread? and your labour for that which satisfieth not? hearken diligently unto me, and eat ye that which is good, and let your soul delight itself in fatness.
> Isaiah 55:2

For weeks, our car had a leaky tire. Every few days, the low-tire-pressure light would go on, and we'd find a free air pump and fill that tire up until it hit 32 pounds per square inch. We knew we needed to get it fixed, but perhaps we were too busy, lazy, or cheap to do it. How long would we keep at this? How long would we keep putting air into a leaky tire?

The prophet Haggai understood this kind of problem, which is typical human nature: "Ye eat, but ye have not enough . . . ye clothe you, but there is none warm; and he that earneth wages earneth wages to put it into a bag with holes. Thus saith the Lord of hosts; Consider your ways" (Haggai 1:6–7). Often, in marriage, we do the same thing with our finances. We put our money into a bag with holes in it, spending it and then wondering where it all went. Sound familiar?

People view money in many different ways. Some come from a lot of money, while others have to scrimp and save their whole lives. Some view it as something to enjoy in the moment, and others would rather "save for the future." Conflicts often come up when one spouse views and spends money differently than the other; in fact, it's one of the most common things couples fight about. But it doesn't matter to the Lord how much money you have. What matters is how you manage it and how you use it to bless others.

Have you ever considered your financial position—as abundant or meager as it may be—as a stewardship? Having a stewardship mentality means that you recognize God as the source of all the good things you enjoy and that your heart is full of gratitude and a desire to use those resources for good. This mentality impacts the way you think and feel about money, which in turn affects what you decide to do with it.

How can this mentality help you avoid the financial challenges that plague and even destroy so many marriages?

First, becoming good stewards requires you to learn to manage your finances. If you don't, those finances will soon be managing you! Second, you and your spouse need to be on the same page when it comes to financial matters. That doesn't mean you have to completely agree on everything—no doubt, a little flexibility is important and can go a long way in maintaining marital harmony—but it does mean that you need to understand one another and work together as you make decisions about your finances and your future.

We recommend holding a monthly finance meeting to review expenditures and make sure you're on the same page. Talk about your current spending habits, and discuss your financial wants and needs. Talk about the specifics of what you're spending money on and why. Set goals for how much you want to save each month, establish and stick to a budget, create long-term goals that unite you, and celebrate your successes together as milestones are achieved.

Learning and practicing sound financial principles will be a great blessing in your marriage. Not only will it help you avoid the pitfalls that often lead to significant stress and conflict, it will also pave the way for a comfortable future where you'll be able to focus your energies on serving and blessing those around you.

FOR DISCUSSION

Use the following agenda to guide your first finance meeting.

Finance Meeting Agenda

1. Pray for insights and creative ideas that will help you reach your financial goals.

2. Discuss how your past experiences have shaped your views on money.

3. Read Proverbs 23:1. As you consider your financial life carefully, what actions do you feel the Lord would have you take?

4. Review your current income and expenditures from the past month. One by one, discuss each item and why you needed it. Make sure you have a tracking system that works to help you keep tabs on your spending.

5. Is your current budget working? If not, what changes need to be made?

6. Review your current debts, and create a plan for how to start paying them down. Make getting out of debt one of your top priorities!

7. What are your short-, medium-, and long-term financial goals? How are you making and tracking your progress toward those goals? Have you celebrated your successes?

8. How have you seen the Lord blessing you as you've been wise and generous stewards over the resources He has blessed you with? How can you be more generous with what you've been given?

9. What can you do to gain new skills, network, and improve your employment opportunities?

10. What else can you be doing to save for retirement, invest wisely, and follow sound financial principles?

11. Close with prayer, thanking God for all that He has blessed you with. Also pray for courage to stick with your plan, to be flexible when necessary, and to be patient and encouraging with each other throughout the process.

God will do *great* things in your life

> For God sent not his Son into the world to condemn the
> world; but that the world through him might be saved.
> John 3:17

Many years ago, April decided she wanted to read the Bible all the way through. She had read parts of it but had never started in Genesis and read all the way to the end. Starting was easy enough to do, but finishing—that was hard. It took her three long and beautiful years. She was steady and consistent, but she also wasn't reading just to finish. She was studying and searching for truth. She went at her own pace and came to understand God and His goodness in a new way.

Before she began her study each day, she committed to looking for and recording the answer to one question: What are the great things that God has done for His children? She found answers on almost every page. Throughout thousands of years of human hardship, there was God: constant, steady, and always ready to help, lift, and love His struggling children.

Through her years of reading the Bible, April learned that God was the same yesterday, today, and forever. The truth taught in Malachi 3:6 is repeated in scripture in different forms and variations, all saying the same thing: "For I am the Lord, I change not." If God did great things in the lives of those who lived before us—if He could help, strengthen, and love Hannah, Moses, Martha, and Timothy—then certainly God could do the same things for us today.

In her reading, April also noted that the great things God has done for His children range from large miracles to quiet instructions and answers to prayers. And there is a single act that is greater than all the rest: sending His Son, Jesus Christ, to be our Savior. Sending Jesus

Christ into our world is the greatest thing that God has done for His children, including you. No matter what challenges, difficulties, or hardships you and your spouse face, no matter how dark and dreary the days seem, because of who He is and what He has done for you, Jesus Christ can and will help you. He can provide the healing and change necessary to restore your marriage.

As she went through this exercise with the Bible, April decided to keep another record, which she has titled, "The Great Things That God Has Done for Me and Our Family." In a journal, she records personal experiences she has that are sacred, special, or inspiring, and the ways she sees God's hand in her life and the lives of loved ones. She tries to write down the great things God is doing in her life, from helping us purchase our first home, to strengthening her during a challenging time, to simply blessing her with all green lights as she rushed to an appointment.

As you come to know God and recognize His hand in your life, your relationship with Him will grow. Individually and in your marriage, you will find access to the power, help, and healing that come from His Son. And as you make a special effort to record and remember how God is blessing you and doing great things in your life, you will be more grateful for those around you, particularly your spouse, and you'll feel His love for both of you in new ways.

FOR DISCUSSION

- How can knowing that God has done great things in the past help you face your difficulties with faith?

- How can seeing that God is already deeply involved in your life fill you with confidence for the future?

- How will recognizing His goodness in your life change you and improve your marital relationship?

- How can recording these great things help you remember them?

FURTHER READING

Read the following scriptures together, and apply them to your life. How do they help you see God's hand in your life?

- Luke 1:49
- 1 Samuel 12:24
- Psalm 106:21
- Psalm 126:3
- Mark 5:19

when someone has been
unfaithful

He that is without sin among you, let him first cast a stone.
John 8:7

This week's scripture passage is not just about a woman "taken in adultery" (John 8:4). It is about all of us. The story is worth revisiting, as the lessons it teaches can help anyone come closer to Christ—and improve their marriage.

The story, as told in John 8:1–11, begins with the Savior at the temple, teaching those who had gathered to hear him, when the Pharisees—a priestly class in Jerusalem at the time—brought in a woman they said they'd caught in the act of adultery.

What a confounding group of people, those Pharisees! They always thought they knew better than Jesus what was godly and right, but they consistently did ungodly things. Yet in their hypocritical ways, we often, surprisingly, see a glimpse of ourselves. We all have lessons to learn from those who think they can find holiness in pointing fingers and assigning blame. These men were probably painfully unprepared for the lesson the Savior would teach them that day.

The Pharisees wanted justice, which to them meant stoning the woman to death. "Now Moses in the law commanded us, that such should be stoned: but what sayest thou?" they asked.

Then we read the Savior's perfect and humbling response: "Jesus stooped down, and with his finger wrote on the ground, as though he heard them not. So when they continued asking him, he lifted up himself, and said unto them, He that is without sin among you, let him first cast a stone at her."

For the first time in a long while, the Pharisees must have realized the painful truth of Jesus' words. They must have looked inward and recognized the pain and error of their own ways. They may not have been caught in adultery, but if they were to stand before a heavenly judge, their sins would still prevent them from being worthy to live with God again. They may have never felt the need for a Savior up until that point, but in that very moment, Jesus Christ taught them how much they each needed Him in order to be saved from sin.

A gentle and humbling miracle occurred. All the people who had condemned this woman for her choice "went out one by one, beginning at the eldest, even unto the last." Isn't it interesting that the oldest ones had their consciences pricked first? Perhaps they more easily recognized some of their own foolish and youthful mistakes. Or perhaps age and experience had worn down their pride a little and replaced it with some humility for the lessons they were once too young and hard-hearted to learn.

Left alone with the woman, Jesus asked her two questions. "Woman, where are those thine accusers? hath no man condemned thee? She said, No man, Lord." Now, pay careful attention to the miracle this woman received when the Savior said, "Neither do I condemn thee: go, and sin no more."

Jesus invited her to change. He invited her to move forward, to be different, to try again, and He gave her a new start. He invites each of us to do the same. We all need the Savior. We all need healing. We all need help being more faithful to ourselves, to God, and to our spouses. As we choose to let the Savior into our hearts, we can enjoy the same peace, forgiveness, and new beginning that this woman's experience so beautifully illustrates.

Navigating infidelity and rebuilding trust isn't easy. And the gift of mercy and forgiveness available through Jesus Christ doesn't negate personal accountability or sometimes painful consequences. But it does make rebuilding possible. The fact that you're reading this book shows that you want to improve your relationship with the Savior and with your spouse. You can experience the miracle of forgiveness, just like the woman in John 8, as you rely on the Savior to sincerely repent, move past your mistakes, and become a new person in Christ.

FOR DISCUSSION

Read Exodus 20:14 and Romans 3:23. Then review John 8 and discuss what you can learn from the accusers, from the woman, and from Jesus.

1. How does this story apply to you and your spouse in your marriage, especially if there have been deep wounds caused by poor decisions?

2. How do you think this woman felt when she looked into the Savior's eyes and heard His words?

3. What do you think happened to those Pharisees that day? What stories would they have told around the dinner table? What changes may have taken place in their hearts?

4. How can you see your spouse the way the Savior does? How can you see your spouse as who they can become, rather than defining them by past mistakes?

5. How can you let the miracle of the Atonement of Jesus Christ change your heart and actions?

giving and receiving

Remember the words of the Lord Jesus, how he said,
It is more blessed to give than to receive.
Acts 20:35

Every day, in hundreds of small ways, you and your spouse are faced with choices about how to give to each other and receive from each other. This isn't quite the same as "taking turns" when you were children because the balance won't always be perfectly equal or fair. It might feel relatively fair in simple tasks like doing the dishes, putting the kids to bed, or picking what to do for date night. But it likely won't be fair when life happens and a spouse has surgery, a baby is born, or a job demands evenings and weekends away from home.

You two are a team. Giving and receiving isn't about keeping a tally or using and abusing the other spouse. When done correctly, in a spirit of mutual concern and selflessness, giving and receiving invites a beautiful connection between spouses that helps true love grow and blossom.

"You can be more effective together than apart. In a truly healthy relationship, we enable each other to accomplish more than we could have done alone."
—Francis & Lisa Chan

You may not feel you have much to give, but you do. You can give time, touch, appreciation, talents, affection, respect, kindness, patience, encouragement, loyalty, hard work, sacrifice, humor, understanding, service, sensitivity, and your whole heart and soul. What can you do to receive what your spouse offers? You can pray for eyes to see what he or she is giving, no matter how imperfect the gift may be. You can express gratitude and appreciation for what your spouse has given you, and you can thoughtfully give back.

This process quickly turns into an upward spiral. The nonstop cycle of giving and receiving will fill your relationship with more connection, unity, and happiness. It will strengthen and motivate you to continue giving your all to your growing and thriving relationship.

One of the most beautiful areas of marriage for this balance to play out is in the sexual relationship between husband and wife. Sex invites you to give your heart, body, and soul to your spouse, and to receive your spouse in return—to love and cherish this incredible individual who has given himself or herself to you. Physical intimacy should be accompanied by the utmost respect, unity, and selflessness you can offer. When you care for each other in this way, you'll feel more comfortable sharing your thoughts and feelings with each other, and that level of intimacy will enhance your ability to give and receive. As you tenderly care for each other, your physical expressions of love will become more heartfelt, and your trust in each other and in your relationship will expand.

Giving invites selflessness, service, and sacrifice into your marriage. Receiving invites humility, love, and appreciation. Both invite respect, loyalty, and unity. As you and your spouse focus on each other, what you can give, and how you can receive, over time you will develop the meaningful and wonderful marriage you've always wanted.

FOR DISCUSSION

- Have you ever given someone a gift and then seen later that they never used it? Have you ever received a gift that you didn't fully appreciate or use? How did it make you feel, what can you learn from those experiences, and how can that apply to your marriage?

- How well are you receiving the gifts of time, service, and attention that your spouse offers to you?

- Read John 3:16 together. What is the greatest gift that God has given to you?

- Consider the ways you've recently given to your spouse. Have you given enough? How can you give more and in more meaningful ways?

- How well are you receiving the gifts and love that your spouse offers you? How can you be a better receiver of that love?

CHALLENGE

Study the topic of giving and receiving in the scriptures this week, and act on any promptings that come to you from the Holy Ghost.

one thing is *needful*

> Martha, Martha, thou art careful and troubled about many things: But one thing is needful: and Mary hath chosen that good part, which shall not be taken away from her.
> Luke 10:41–42

We love the story of Mary and Martha, perhaps because it's so relatable, or perhaps because it's an experience everyday people had with Jesus Christ. Or perhaps we love this story because it's packed with so many wonderful lessons, all of which are applicable to marriage.

In Luke 10:38–42, we read how Jesus, as he traveled around preaching, stopped at a house inhabited by two sisters named Mary and Martha. While Mary listened to Jesus teach, Martha was busy serving food and otherwise hosting their guests. When she asked Jesus to tell her sister to help her out, He responded with this week's scripture passage. Essentially, He was telling Martha that one thing was needful, and it wasn't the food.

One of the many lessons in this story is that everyone has a bit of Mary and a bit of Martha in them and that our choices and priorities affect our relationships.

The Martha in us is often anxious and busy with in-the-moment concerns. What is troubling you or getting in the way of you having a more connected marriage? Is it a busy schedule or long hours at work? Putting the kids in one too many activities? Or extra home projects that are important but not urgent? Those are the concerns of your inner Martha.

On the other hand, the Mary in us wants to know and choose what's most important. What is the "one thing that is needful" in your marriage today? It may be that your spouse needs you to listen to them. Your spouse may need you to not jump to conclusions or to kiss and cuddle them. Learning what's actually important in your marriage on a day-to-day basis is one of the greatest skills you can develop. The best way to do that is to be sensitive, pay attention, and listen to the quiet promptings of the Holy Ghost. As you do these things, your Heavenly Father will give you inspiration and practical ideas for how to improve your marriage and bless your spouse.

Finally, the story of Mary and Martha also reminds us that the one thing that is most needful in every marriage is Jesus Christ. When a couple centers their lives on Christ and seeks to know and follow Him, their marriage significantly changes, from the way they view and speak to each other to the way they navigate conflict to the connection they share and the ways they nurture love.

Like Mary and Martha, you and your spouse have many stresses and demands on your time. But with the Savior at the center of your life, you'll be able to prioritize correctly, live in line with your value system, and enjoy a more rewarding and connected marriage.

FOR DISCUSSION

As you study the story of Mary and Martha together, individually make a list of 10 things you're "careful and troubled about."

- What's weighing down upon you? What are you worried about? Share your lists with each other and counsel together about each item. This will invite you to open your hearts to each other and be more vulnerable. How can you eliminate some of these stressors from your life so that you aren't cumbered like Martha?

- Cross off two things from your list that aren't needful. What can you let go of? What adds light and life to your marriage? What doesn't?

- Then, look at each other's lists and decide on one thing you can each do to help the other this week.

- Finally, consider what one thing is needful in order to receive the Savior into your life this week. Write it down, make a plan for how to implement it, and commit to making change happen in your relationship.

choosing to be *content*

> Let your conversation be without covetousness; and be content with such things as ye have: for he hath said, I will never leave thee, nor forsake thee.
> Hebrews 13:5

We have often pondered what a blessing it is to be married and the miracle of how God led us together. Truly, isn't it lucky anyone gets married in the first place? That we find someone who wants to live and do life with us? Of course, getting married is the easy part. Staying happily married is what takes a lot more work, effort, and heart.

One of Satan's great tools is to try to convince us that who we are and what we have isn't enough. He wants us to be unhappy with ourselves, our spouses, and our lives—to be ungrateful for what we have. He tries to get us to fantasize about what we *could* have and unhappily compare it to the reality of what we *do* have.

The 10th commandment that God gave to Moses was "Thou shalt not covet thy neighbour's house, thou shalt not covet thy neighbour's wife . . . nor any thing that is thy neighbour's" (Exodus 20:17). Obviously, this feeling of looking sideways, comparing, and being discontent with your lot in life is a human frailty. Bill got a new car, so somehow we need a new car. Sarah and John seem to have a perfect marriage—why don't we?

As easy as it is to fall into the constant-comparison trap, you'll only ever be truly happy when your life is in line with the teachings of Jesus. He can change the way you experience life. With Him by your side, your spouse, family, career, and health will be sources of joy and contentment, not frustration and restlessness.

If, for a time, things aren't quite as you'd hope in your marriage, trust God, and keep putting one foot in front of the other. Things will get better as you make a consistent effort together to improve. Would the other option—giving up on your marriage—really be better? Or would you find new things to be discontent about as you traded one set of problems and challenges for another?

That's not to say that you should live in a bubble and simply pretend things are wonderful if they're not. A small measure of dissatisfaction can be good if it motivates you to make changes to improve your current situation. But if that dissatisfaction only encourages you to give up on the things that really matter, then it doesn't come from God. So strive for the kind of "divine discontentedness" that motivates inspired and positive progress, rather than discouraging and destructive jealousy.

God wants you to be happy, but He also wants you to *choose* happiness, no matter your life circumstances. He would have you see the good in every little thing—especially your spouse. As you see all the things your spouse is doing right and all the love they're trying to give, it will be easier to trust that in time your relationship will become all that you hope for it to become. God will be able to work wonders for you, guiding you along and consecrating your hardships for your gain. As you live in gratitude daily, His goodness, influence, and love will be apparent to you, and you will experience the joy of contentment in every area of your life—especially in your marriage.

FOR DISCUSSION

Together, read the following scriptures:

- Philippians 4:11–13
- 1 Timothy 6:6–12
- Matthew 6:33
- Luke 12:15
- James 1:2–4

- What do these passages teach about contentment and gratitude? Why does Satan use covetousness to distract us? How can gratitude change your perspective on your current relationship and breathe new life into your marriage? What are you most grateful for about each other?

- Take some time to reflect on the story of your relationship. How did you see God's hand bringing you together? What did you dream your future would be like together? How did you view your spouse in the beginning? What did you do for each other? How can you start to do some of the things you used to do to win each other's hearts and give love a chance to blossom anew?

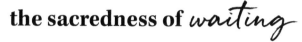

the sacredness of waiting

Wait on the Lord: be of good courage, and he shall
strengthen thine heart: wait, I say, on the Lord.
Psalm 27:14

We live in an age of instant gratification. When we have a question, we can
find immediate answers online. When we want to buy something, we can
order it with the click of a button. We're increasingly unwilling to wait, and
sometimes it seems like we've practically lost the virtue of patience.

Yet life still requires a lot of waiting—not just in traffic or in lines, but
in more meaningful ways, too. Regardless of our desire for immediate
answers or progress, waiting is not always bad. In fact, sometimes it's in
the waiting that we experience the most growth. Whatever circumstances
you find yourself waiting in, take this week's scripture to heart.

In marriage, you've each had to wait for certain things: solutions, apolo-
gies, forgiveness, healing, change. You may still be waiting to feel fully loved,
wanted, needed, and cared about. Unfortunately, not all the desires of your
heart can be purchased online with same-day shipping. But that doesn't
mean that God isn't mindful of those desires and eagerly waiting to bless you.

God has a reason for all these delays. They let you exercise greater
faith in Him, His way, His will, and His timing, and they help develop
patience—an attribute that is essential to having a successful, lasting
marriage. Growing in patience will help you become more Christlike
and, in turn, make you a better spouse, friend, parent, neighbor, and
overall human being.

Waiting can be a test of sorts, requiring the very best you have to offer.
What you choose to do with your waiting period may be just as important
as what you were waiting for all along. Your time need not go to waste;
you can be improving, changing, overcoming, and helping others along the
way. When you find yourself waiting, pray about what God wants you to

learn, do, and become during this period. Then, give yourself to the Lord. As you give Him your very best time and energy, your wait for His help and healing in your life will seem more joyful and easier to bear.

It's also helpful to remember that waiting goes both ways. As Isaiah 30:18 says, "And therefore will the Lord wait, that he may be gracious unto you." God is waiting for you to be humble, to seek His help, and to obey His counsel. He is waiting for you to step up, show up, and do what you came to earth to do. He is also waiting for the right time and way to bless you because He knows best what you need and how to provide for you.

You can trust the Lord—His timing, purpose, and objectives. He wants to help you and your spouse grow, find joy, and create a more connected, fulfilling, and beautiful marriage. Eventually, your waiting period will end. If you have used your wait to draw closer to God, you may find that who you have become, how your faith has grown, and what you have offered to others and to the Lord is more important and valuable than whatever you were waiting for in the first place.

FOR DISCUSSION

Read Luke 1–2 together.

- What can you learn about waiting from the example of Zacharias and Elizabeth in Luke 1?

- What did Zacharias and Elizabeth each wait for? How did they wait? How do you suppose they were blessed for waiting?

- How does this passage make you feel about your personal waiting?

- How might this example change your attitude toward waiting?

- What experiences have you had waiting upon the Lord? What did you learn?

- How will you choose to respond when God's timeline is different than yours?

- What are you currently waiting for?

- What will you do as you wait upon the Lord and trust in His ways and in His timing?

remembering your true *identity*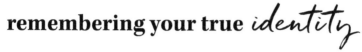

For in him we live, and move, and have our being;
as certain also of your own poets have said, For we
are also his offspring.
Acts 17:28

When April was young, a church leader taught her and her friends
to introduce themselves by saying their names and then the following
statement: "I am a daughter of God. He loves me, and I love Him."
It was something they only did at church, and she's never actually intro-
duced herself by saying that, but the lesson has stayed with her all of
these years. *I am a child of God. He knows my name. He loves me. I love Him.*
Knowing those truths has changed her life.

You are a child of God, too. He loves you. He knows your name.
He has a plan for your life and great things for you to accomplish. He
also knows your spouse. He knows how you two fell in love, how you've
grown, and how you've struggled. He knows the concerns of your
heart, the burdens you bear, and the potential you have to progress and
become. The psalmist said it best when he said, "All of you are children
of the most High" (Psalm 82:6). God loves you and cares about you
because He is your Father.

In Max Lucado's children's book, *You Are Special,* a wooden man
lives in a village of wooden people who give each other stickers to
indicate value and approval. The popular people have many gold
stars while the not-so-popular people, including this man, are covered
in gray dots. One day, the man meets a woman with neither stars nor
dots. They simply don't stick to her. It turns out this is because every
day she visits the woodcarver who created them, and as she spends
time with him, he reminds her of her great value. He helps her know
who she is and *whose* she is, so other people's stickers are meaningless

to her. As a result of hearing her story, the wooden man chooses to visit the woodcarver daily as well, to learn who he is and how the love of his creator can forever change his life.

Like the man in this story, each of us is a child of God, created in His image, and we need to spend time with Him in scripture study, prayer, worship, and service. Knowing that you and your spouse are children of God should change and improve your relationship and how you treat each other. When you're confident about who you are and whose you are, you naturally want to act accordingly. The Adversary, on the other hand, would have you forget who you are and what you came to earth to do. He wants you to dislike yourself and to never feel like you'll measure up. Don't fall for his lies. Instead, remember and focus on the eternal worth of all of God's children.

As you grow in confidence, remember your identity as God's child, and feel His love for you, you'll be better able to help your spouse remember who they are as well. There will be times when your spouse will need a boost after a blow to their confidence at work, a crushing health diagnosis, or simply a bad day. In these situations, do all you can to love your spouse and demonstrate how valuable they are to you. When you see your spouse the way God does and help them see it, too, great things will happen. The unity, love, purpose, and mission you share will bless your marriage and help you accomplish the great things that God has in store for you.

FOR DISCUSSION

- When have you felt that you were your most confident self? What factors contributed to this feeling of confidence?

- What experiences have helped you feel loved and valued in God's eyes? Share these experiences with each other, and listen with love.

- How will knowing that you're a son or daughter of God, and that you were born for more, change the choices you make?

- Do you know what your personal mission is? What were you born to do? Who were you born to be? What are you and your spouse supposed to accomplish together? Write down three things that you each think should be on that list, and then share your thoughts with each other.

- How will seeing your spouse as a child of God help you refrain from being critical, nagging, or controlling, and instead be encouraging, uplifting, and supportive?

- What can you do to encourage, support, and help your spouse grow in his or her identity and purpose as a child of God? How will you help each other in these sacred and important pursuits?

the power of your *words*

Let no corrupt communication proceed out of your mouth, but that which is good to the use of edifying, that it may minister grace unto the hearers.
Ephesians 4:29

Many years ago, April read the verse for this devotion and decided that for 24 hours she wasn't going to let "corrupt communication" proceed out of her mouth. It wasn't easy. She wanted to complain multiple times but instead chose to focus on the positive. The people she talked to that day might have thought she was overly optimistic, but she had a great day. She recognized the power of her words and only wishes she could report that she's been diligent about that goal ever since.

When avoiding corrupt communication with your spouse, the words you speak matter, as do the tone and volume of your voice. The same words can convey very different messages depending on the emotion behind them. When you carefully manage both your words and your tone, you'll be far more effective at communicating, and your message is less likely to be misinterpreted. Couples who master this skill are able to discuss just about anything without causing offense or hurt feelings.

How can you do this? Start by speaking in a measured tone, and avoid raising your voice or yelling. There are few things that stir up contention faster than raising your voice and talking over one another. In addition, avoid speaking in absolutes. Rather than saying, "You always do this" or "You never do that," try expressing your feelings by saying, "When _____ happens, I feel _____."

But avoiding the negative repercussions of poor communication isn't enough. Your marriage needs positive and uplifting communication in order to thrive. Train yourself to make kind and encouraging remarks—to praise, compliment, and point out the good you see in your spouse. As you use your words to lift, strengthen, and respect your spouse, you will truly "minister grace unto the hearers," and your marriage will be better for it.

Here are a few suggestions for how to improve the communication in your marriage.

NEGATIVE COMMUNICATION SKILLS TO AVOID

Criticism/blame. It's all too easy to blame others for your problems, but it rarely accomplishes anything. As much as you may want to point out the things you believe your spouse is doing wrong, don't. Bite your tongue, and find a more tactful way to communicate your observations.

Attacking. Verbally attacking your significant other is a poor way to start any conversation and will achieve little good. If your spouse says something that rubs you the wrong way, avoid reacting mindlessly. Instead, take the moral high ground, and select your response carefully and maturely.

Complaining. It's important to be able to communicate your needs, frustrations, and feelings, but nonstop complaining is not an effective way of doing that. Look on the bright side, and find all that you have to be grateful for first.

Name-calling. When you've been hurt, it can be easy to fall into name-calling as a way to demean or "get back at" your spouse. But that will never improve the situation. Using mean or hurtful words will only make things worse. So be wise.

Lying. When you lie to your spouse—even little white lies—you start down a slippery slope. One lie leads to the next, and before you know it, you're caught in a trap that you laid for yourself. But even more important is the fact that lies destroy trust, and trust is critical to a fulfilling marriage.

POSITIVE COMMUNICATION SKILLS TO PRACTICE

Attitude. Choose to have a positive attitude, and speak constructively about yourself, your spouse, and your marriage. Focus on the good things that are happening in your relationship, and specifically point out things you are grateful for.

Validation. Your spouse needs to know you care about how they feel. When your spouse expresses a frustration or unmet need, listen carefully and validate their feelings. Say something like "that must really be hard" or "I can imagine how frustrated you must feel."

Praise. Praise, compliment, and thank your spouse for every good thing you see. Point out why you appreciate what your spouse does and what you love about them.

Apologize/forgive. When you've done something that hurt your spouse, be quick to apologize. When your spouse has done something to hurt you, be quick to forgive. "I'm sorry, I love you" and "That's okay, I love you, too" are two very powerful phrases.

Respect. Making eye contact, putting away distractions, and considering your spouse's opinion all communicate respect. Pay attention to the way you speak to and about your spouse, and seek to honor your spouse and treat them as the most important person around.

Honesty. When you speak the truth (always in kindness!) and don't hide things from your spouse, you build trust and strengthen the foundation of your relationship.

If you and your spouse have been fighting a lot or saying hurtful things to each other, don't lose hope. Becoming a good communicator doesn't happen overnight. It takes practice and patience. But as you use these tips and seek God's help with carefully selecting your words and tone of voice, you'll avoid corrupt communication and minister grace to each other, which will bless your marriage and help you both feel safe, loved, and respected.

FOR DISCUSSION

- Reread the positive communication skills listed earlier, and circle one thing your spouse is extremely good at. Share your thoughts and appreciation with your spouse.

- Share experiences you have had in the past where someone's words lifted and strengthened you. How did those words help you feel loved, validated, or encouraged?

- What is one specific thing you can work on as a couple to improve the communication in your marriage? Commit to practicing this skill this week.

CHALLENGE

Take the 24-hour challenge to avoid corrupt communication for one full day. Instead, choose to communicate with each other in ways that invite the Spirit and strengthen your marriage.

the Lord will *help* you

Fear thou not; for I am with thee: be not dismayed; for I am thy God: I will strengthen thee; yea, I will help thee; yea, I will uphold thee with the right hand of my righteousness . . . For I the Lord thy God will hold thy right hand, saying unto thee, Fear not; I will help thee.
Isaiah 41:10, 13

We often see anniversary posts on social media, celebrating the years couples have spent together. These posts tend to be flattering, expressing the best that spouses see in each other. But occasionally they share a more realistic glimpse into the ups and downs that inevitably come to all those who venture down the path of marriage.

You may have been on this marriage journey for three years, 15 years, or 44 years. In that period of time, you and your spouse have lived, loved, laughed, cried, worked, played, struggled, succeeded, and faced plenty of challenges together. Certainly, in every marriage, there are hardships that weigh upon the minds and hearts of good husbands and wives. These difficulties can be frustrating or even overwhelming as you struggle to maintain and grow your relationship with each other, with your children, and with God.

Marriage has likely presented you with many an opportunity to feel like giving up. But on those days when working on the relationship seems too hard, and when all you can see is everything that's going wrong in your marriage, remember the words of Isaiah 50:9: "Behold, the Lord God will help me." That positive affirmation and statement of faith is true. God *will* help you. And He *will* help your spouse and your marriage. You simply have to ask for that help.

o He will help you when you're angry at your spouse for doing something you thought was wrong.

o He will help you when one of you gets laid off and the stress of finances weighs upon you both.

o He will help you when you feel discouraged, depressed, and desolate.

o He will help you have the courage to say no to some of the extra demands on your time that are causing you unnecessary stress.

o He will help you respond with patience and understanding when your spouse shares their frustrations with you.

o He will help you with difficult decisions.

o He will help you withstand the temptations that seek to pull you down.

o He will help you and your spouse learn to find solutions together without fighting and distancing yourselves from each other.

o He will help you forgive and forget.

o He will help you see and love your spouse the way He does.

o He will help your marriage become everything you've ever hoped it would be.

When you find yourselves overwhelmed with the burdens of life, remember that there is a purpose to these challenges. They will shape you, refine you, and help you come unto Christ—if you let them. He *wants* to help you. It's not a question of *if* the Lord will help you, but rather *when* you'll reach out to Him for His help.

So never feel like you're in this alone. Marriage is not just a two-way partnership. When we include God (as He invites us to), it's a three-way partnership. Tapping into His infinite love and power can make all the difference in creating a connected, meaningful, and even sacred marriage.

FOR DISCUSSION

- List three specific things you need God's help with, either individually or in your marriage. Why do you need His help with these things? What actions can you take so that God can better help you have a more joy-filled marriage?

- What stories from the scriptures come to mind that teach you that God has always helped His children?

- In what specific ways has God helped you, individually and as a couple, in the past?

- How can you access His help? How will you recognize it when it comes? And how will you give thanks for it as you receive it? Write down any thoughts or ideas that come to mind. These may be ways you can begin to access His help this week.

the beauty of mature *love*

> And let us not be weary in well doing: for in due season
> we shall reap, if we faint not.
> Galatians 6:9

It's easy to pick out couples who are newly in love—the constant kissing, teasing, doting on each other. You know the type. You may roll your eyes at the sight, but you may also quietly wonder where the romance went in your marriage. How did you two go from starry-eyed lovers to where you are now? When did you stop wanting to be together every second of the day, and how do you suddenly have nothing to say to each other on the phone? Where have those romantic feelings gone, and is it possible to ever get them back?

Before you beat yourself up or wonder if you married the wrong person, remember that this is normal. As the chime of wedding bells dies down, so, too, do some of the butterfly feelings of *young* love. Nevertheless, if you continually nurture your marriage, it can blossom into an even more meaningful and wonderful *mature* love, the kind of love that God always intended for His children.

Marriage is meant to be more than a constant state of infatuation. God intends for you and your spouse to walk through life together, to cre-ate a family, and to share the ups, downs, and in betweens of real life as loyal and devoted partners. He intends for you to learn what committed, mature love is. While mature love is different from newlywed bliss, it's far from boring and certainly doesn't lack energy or romance.

If you find yourself somewhat jealous of those newlyweds and you want to increase the romance in your relationship, focus on doing the small things that grow love. For example, try doing some of the things you did back when you were dating. Revisiting those activities and locations will remind you of your own love story and can reignite those butterfly feelings. In addition, give your spouse more of your time and attention. Find ways to express your love through word and deed. Laugh a little more. Forgive quickly. Be physically affectionate. See the best in each other. Make time for dating. Don't be embarrassed to let the world know you love each other.

Love is built one kind deed at a time. The real spark of romance isn't ignited just by roses on Valentine's Day or passionate nights in bed. Rather, it comes from consistent devotion, loyalty, and selflessness as you and your spouse serve each other. Real romance comes from confronting hardships with faith, harsh words with forgiveness, and trials with unity. This real romance or mature love blossoms as patience, forgiveness, thoughtfulness, selflessness, and service become everyday realities in your relationship.

As you make intentional efforts to nurture your marriage, you'll get to experience the beauty of mature love. Those romantic feelings will return, and this time they'll be accompanied by deeper and more sincere feelings of concern, kindness, and a desire to lift and serve your spouse. Where you once felt distant from your spouse, you'll find that a unity of purpose has closed the gap. Where you once lacked affection, you'll find a rekindled flame for emotional and physical intimacy. Where you once experienced frustration and even anger, you'll find increased patience and understanding.

As you carefully nurture your marriage through little things each and every day, you'll experience the beauty of mature and enduring love and recognize it as one of God's greatest gifts to you.

FOR DISCUSSION

- What do 2 Timothy 2:22 and the scripture beginning this week's devotional teach you about the difference between new love and the beauty of mature love?

- What are your greatest desires for your marriage?

- Is there anything you need to change to enable you to experience mature love in your marriage? If so, what can you do differently, and how will you make the change?

- How will you stay committed to the process even if you don't see or feel immediate results?

- Why is time a necessary factor in growing mature love?

CHALLENGE

Review your wedding vows, place them where they can be seen daily, and plan a time to renew them soon.

the greatest *champion* of your marriage

What shall we then say to these things? If God be for us, who can be against us?
Romans 8:31

God intends for your marriage to last forever. That's a long time, but don't feel daunted; 2 Kings 6:8–23 tells a great story about how God champions your marriage and sends help today, tomorrow, and forever.

The great prophet Elisha was guiding the king of Israel in a war against Syria—as a seer, he could tell what the Syrian king was planning to do next. Well, the Syrian king didn't like that, and when he found out that Elisha was staying in the city of Dothan, he sent "horses, and chariots, and a great host" who "compassed the city about" looking for the prophet.

Imagine how it would feel to wake up and find yourself surrounded by the Syrian army, as Elisha and his servant did. Pretty intimidating. Maybe a similar feeling to the ones you've had when facing difficult situations in your marriage?

Let's see how the story unfolds.

Elisha's servant understandably panicked, crying, "Alas, my master! How shall we do?" But Elisha could see and understand more than this servant, and he said, with a great deal of calm and faith, "Fear not: for they that be with us are more than they that be with them." Then something miraculous happened: "Elisha prayed, and said, Lord, I pray thee, open his eyes, that he may see. And the Lord opened the eyes of the young man; and he saw: and, behold, the mountain was full of horses and chariots of fire round about Elisha."

The servant hadn't known that he and Elisha were surrounded and protected by God's angels. He hadn't realized the help that was available but unseen. Perhaps he hadn't realized the grandness and goodness of a God in heaven who cares deeply about and knows each of His children. But that day he learned about the nature, character, and goodness of God, and also about faith, miracles, and heavenly help. The story concludes as the prophet Elisha is given power to blind the soldiers, lead them to a different city, feed them a meal, and then peacefully send them back to Syria with their sight restored.

We love that story, especially its application to marriage. We are certain there are angels, seen and unseen, who will be instruments in the hands of God to come and help you in your marriage. We hope these words from Jeffrey R. Holland encourage you when, spiritually speaking, it feels as though an army has surrounded you, your marriage is in danger, and you're unsure of what to do.

"If we give our heart to God, if we love the Lord Jesus Christ . . . then tomorrow—and every other day—is ultimately going to be magnificent, even if we don't always recognize it as such. Why? Because our Heavenly Father wants it to be! . . . So keep loving. Keep trying. Keep trusting . . . Heaven is cheering you on today, tomorrow, and forever."

Heaven is not only cheering; God is sending help in the form of protection, encouragement, resources, friends, family members, and more—even if, like Elisha's servant, you can't always see it. Certainly hard times will come to every married couple, but with God by your side, you will not just get through it but also *grow* through it and become better and happier because of it.

Whatever you do and wherever you are in your relationship, don't give up. God will bless and magnify every effort you make to let Him into your marriage, because marriage is ordained by Him. He is the greatest champion of your marriage and the missing link to your happily ever after.

FOR DISCUSSION

- How does knowing that God is the greatest champion of your marriage make you feel? How does it affect the way you approach the current struggles you face in your marriage?

- How have you seen God's hand in your life? In your marriage?

- In what ways has God opened your eyes to the miracles around you and the help and resources He provides?

- Prayerfully ask God, "What shall we do?" and then listen. Act on promptings that come and decide on one thing you can do this week to not only open your eyes to God's goodness and involvement in your life and in your marriage, but to help you take one step in the right direction toward a marriage approved and championed by God.

what God intends *marriage* to be

As for God, his way is perfect . . . It is God that girdeth me
with strength, and maketh my way perfect.
Psalm 18:30, 32

In marriage, we often have expectations for how things should be, how
our spouse should act, or what we should be getting out of a relationship. We so quickly forget that God has a bigger plan for marriage than
just romance, attraction, meeting needs, or learning to communicate
(though those things are, of course, super important). Learning to see
God's plan for marriage may make all the difference for you. God didn't
put us in marriages and families to watch us fail. He did it precisely
because marriage is the perfect institution for you and your spouse to
grow, change, improve, and make progress—to become the people you
all hope to become.

There will be moments when you say, "This isn't happily ever after."
Well, maybe that *moment* isn't, but that doesn't mean you're on the wrong
path. Maybe the fairy-tale kind of love we all want isn't about being happy
24/7. Maybe it's about *choosing* to be happy through the experiences that
help us learn, grow, and become, painful though they may be.

In marriage, we often have to soften our hearts and recognize that
things may not be what we expected or planned for, but they are perfect
for us because they provide the very opportunities God intended marriage
to provide. You aren't perfect, and your spouse isn't perfect. Your marriage isn't perfect—but it's perfect for you when you understand what God
intended it to be. Consider:

- If your marriage has provided you with the opportunity to practice
  patience, forgiveness, and love, then it is what God intended it to be.

- If your marriage has taught you about true love, about lasting love,
  and about enduring love, then it is what God intended it to be.

- If your marriage has required of you sacrifice, hard work, and humility, then it is what God intended it to be.
- If your marriage has invited you to look inward, put away your proud heart, and turn toward your spouse and family, then it is what God intended it to be.
- If your marriage has invited you to focus on not just your own interests, hobbies, and goals, but on the progress of your spouse and children, then it is what God intended it to be.
- If your marriage has shown you that your way isn't always the right way and that God's ways are higher than your ways, then it is what God intended it to be.
- If your marriage has required you to give your time, your energy, and your very heart to people who haven't always loved you perfectly, then it is what God intended it to be.
- If your marriage has helped you see and value someone else the way that He does, then it is what God intended it to be.
- If your marriage has provided you with opportunities to be a team and to combine your strengths in order to have greater capacity to lift, serve, and help others, then it is what God intended it to be.
- If your marriage has invited you individually and as a couple to turn to the Savior for help, healing, wholeness, and happiness, then it is exactly what God intended it to be.

God intended for your marriage to change you—your heart, your attitudes, your habits, your desires, your aim and focus in life. While happiness isn't the only objective, it is a natural result of a heart that is changing and becoming more like His. Happiness in married life is the result of living a God-centered life, relying on Christ, and following the guidance of the Holy Spirit

Marriage is ordained by God. It is supported by Him, championed by Him, and approved by Him. God intends for His children to return home to Him as families—as husbands, wives, and children.

As you have spent the past year working through this devotional, we hope that your hearts have been changed in Christ and that you're beginning to experience the growth and healing that you've been praying and working for. Your marriage may still not be perfect, but Jesus Christ is, and with His help, your marriage can be all that God intends for it to be. We testify that, as the Savior of the world, He can save your marriage. And your marriage is worth saving. Through Him, your marriage will be perfect for you and perfect in fulfilling its intended purposes in God's great eternal plan of happiness for His children.

FOR DISCUSSION

Read Psalm 19:7, Matthew 19:21, John 17:23, and Colossians 3:14, and consider how they apply to your marriage right now. Share your thoughts and feelings with each other and then answer the following questions.

o What will change for you when you realize that marriage and family life are meant to invite growth and change and not just happiness and pleasure?

o In what ways are your spouse and your marriage perfect for you?

o How will coming unto Christ and letting Him into your marriage show you that His way is perfect and that through Him, your marriage can be, too?

GOING FORWARD

Congratulations! You have successfully and diligently worked through this book of devotions. But this is just the beginning of a wonderful journey to deepen your love for each other and to let God lead and bless you in your marriage.

As you think back on the past year together, we hope you have found hope, healing, encouragement, and practical guidance to help your relationship.

○ Which was your favorite devotion and why?

○ What is one lesson or thought that particularly touched you as you read this book?

○ How have you changed as you've read and applied the teachings in this book?

○ What is the most important thing you've learned this year?

○ What do you feel inspired to do?

We're confident that as you continue to be diligent students, and as you seek insight and knowledge from the right sources, God will bless you in your efforts. This book has taught you a pattern of seeking truth in the scriptures and learning to receive personal inspiration for your lives. We hope that in this book you two found growth, insight, and wisdom as you dug a little deeper, read scriptures together, discussed principles, and applied what you were learning to your lives.

In the coming weeks and months, revisit this devotional. Keep your copy on your nightstand and open it up from time to time to remind yourselves of the lessons you've learned. We hope inspiration, encouragement, and success will be yours as you apply these truths to your marriage for years to come.

True restoration only happens in and through Jesus Christ. He can and will work miracles in your marriage, if you let Him. He'll heal old wounds and fill you with faith and hope. He'll help you learn the skills necessary to communicate with respect, to love and serve your spouse better, and to build a trusting relationship. Yes, forgiveness, renewal, and restoration are all gifts that can be yours through Christ. We know and testify that He is real and that His power can forever change your marriage if you will just invite Him in.

FIND MARRIAGE MENTORS

God has placed certain people in your life for a reason. One of the best ways that God blesses us, guides us, and encourages us is through others. In that vein, we love to find couples whom we look up to and invite them to dinner. Sometimes we let them know that we want to pick their brains about a particular topic, and sometimes we simply take them out, observe, and learn all we can from them.

We encourage you to find your own marriage mentors— people who champion marriage and who will offer heartfelt advice and encouragement if you're ever feeling down. God will place the right people in your path and provide you with the support and help you need to restore and rebuild your relationship through Christ.

I am the light of the world: he
that followeth me shall not walk
in darkness, but shall have the
light of life.

JOHN 8:12

ADDITIONAL RESOURCES

Here's a list of resources we love that are both practical and Spirit-filled. We encourage you to spend time checking out each resource together, paying attention to which ones you're drawn to. God will inspire you to find the support necessary to help you restore and rebuild your marriage in and through Christ. We're sure of it.

Nurturing Marriage (**NurturingMarriage.org**)
On our website, we post articles, interviews, and videos that focus on practical tips for taking care of your marriage and bringing the romance back. Our six pillars to nurturing marriage include The Little Things, Date Night, Intimacy, Values to Live By, Routines and Rituals, and Conflict Resolution.

Nurture: 100 Practical Tips for Marriage by April and Aaron Jacob
A simple, fast read, our first book provides practical advice and ideas to help you start nurturing your marriage today. These hands-on tips will help lead you to the deeply connected, highly meaningful, and very satisfying marriage you've always wanted.

The Five Love Languages by Gary Chapman
We encourage you to read this book as a couple (and take the quiz online) in order to better understand each other's needs and how to express your love to each other in the right "love language."

The Seven Principles for Making Marriage Work by John Gottman, PhD, and Nan Silver
Dr. John Gottman is a world-renowned marriage and relationship expert, and this book contains his research, boiled down into seven important principles. A must-read for every couple who wants their marriage to work!

His Needs, Her Needs by Willard F. Harley Jr.
This book dives into the top 10 needs that most husbands and wives have and discusses how to meet those needs within your marriage so you don't start looking elsewhere.

You Need a Budget (YouNeedABudget.com)
Award-winning software (plus an app) that will help you stop living paycheck to paycheck, get out of debt, and save more money.

Addo Recovery (AddoRecovery.com)
Specialized therapy for couples dealing with sexual addiction, betrayal, trauma, and infidelity. Locations all over the United States and Canada.

Spouse and Family Support Guide
Find a free PDF guide offering support for spouses and family of those in recovery at https://addictionrecovery.lds.org/spouses-and-families.

The Book of Mormon: Another Testament of Jesus Christ
A companion to the Bible, this book of scripture teaches and testifies about Christ and helps individuals, couples, and families draw closer to God and feel His love in their lives. Request a free copy at www.mormon .org/free-book-of-mormon.

REFERENCES

Ballard, M. Russell. "Daughters of God." LDS.org. April 2008. https://www.lds.org/general-conference/2008/04/daughters-of-god.

Chan, Francis, and Lisa Chan. *You and Me Forever: Marriage in Light of Eternity*. San Francisco: Claire Love Publishing, 2014.

Craig, Michelle D. "Divine Discontent." LDS.org. October 2018. https://www.lds.org/general-conference/2018/10/divine-discontent ?lang=eng.

Doherty, William J. *The Intentional Family: Simple Rituals to Strengthen Family Ties.* New York: Quill, 2002.

Fairchild, Mary. "Biography of Corrie ten Boom, Hero of the Holocaust." ThoughtCo. Last modified July 7, 2018. https://www.thoughtco.com/biography-of-corrie-ten-boom-4164625.

Hales, Robert D. "Holy Scriptures: The Power of God unto Our Salvation." LDS.org. October 2006. https://www.lds.org/general-conference /2006/10/holy-scriptures-the-power-of-god-unto-our-salvation?lang=eng.

Holland, Jeffrey R. "Tomorrow the Lord Will Do Wonders among You." LDS.org. April 2016. https://www.lds.org/general-conference/2016/04 /tomorrow-the-lord-will-do-wonders-among-you.

Holland, Matthew. "Wrong Roads and Revelation." LDS.org. July 2005. https://www.lds.org/new-era/2005/07/wrong-roads-and-revelation ?lang=eng.

Hunter, Howard W. "Reading the Scriptures." LDS.org. Accessed December 16, 2018. https://www.lds.org/general-conference/1979/10/reading-the-scriptures.

Lucado, Max. *You Are Special*. Wheaton, IL: Crossway Books, 1997.

Monson, Thomas S. "Choices." LDS.org. April 2016. https://www.lds.org/general-conference/2016/04/choices.

Robbins, Lynn G. "Avoid It." BYU Speeches. September 17, 2003. https://speeches.byu.edu/talks/lynn-g-robbins_avoid/.

Smith, Jennifer. *Wife After God: Drawing Closer to God & Your Husband*. Smith Family Resources, Inc: 2016.

The First Presidency and Council of the Twelve Apostles of The Church of Jesus Christ of Latter-day Saints. "The Family: A Proclamation to the World." LDS.org. September 23, 1995. https://www.lds.org/topics/family-proclamation.

Thomas, Gary. *Sacred Marriage: What If God Designed Marriage to Make Us Holy More Than to Make Us Happy?* Grand Rapids, MI: Zondervan, 2000.

VERSES INDEX

OLD TESTAMENT

NEW TESTAMENT

INDEX

ACKNOWLEDGMENTS

We couldn't have written this book on our own—and we didn't. We want to thank a few friends who helped along the way and made this possible. If this book helps you in any way, it is due to the work and effort of many individuals.

We want to acknowledge the work of Callisto Media, with special mention to Elizabeth Castoria, who convinced us to write this book, and Nana K. Twumasi, our fabulous and dedicated editor. A huge thank you to everyone on the team who took this idea and turned it into a reality.

We want to acknowledge dear friends and family members whose thoughts and conversations have sparked ideas shared in this book.

We want to thank our *Nurturing Marriage* community for their support and their commitment to nurturing and improving their own marriages.

Our hearts are most thankful for our three sons, Michael, Thomas, and Jonathan, who have patiently supported us as we've focused on this book for a season. We love you, boys.

Finally, we are thankful for you, our community of readers. We have prayed for you and thought about you as we've written this book. We want your marriages to succeed. We want you to find the peace that only Christ can bring to your relationship. And we want you to enjoy opening your hearts to each other as you study these devotions together. Thank you for being here and for taking the time to read this book.

ABOUT THE AUTHORS

Aaron and April Jacob are the authors of the book, *Nurture: 100 Practical Tips for Marriage*, and the founders of *Nurturing Marriage* (www.NurturingMarriage.org), a website dedicated to offering practical advice to help strengthen marriages and families everywhere. They have spoken at numerous retreats and conferences, been featured on TV and talk radio, and published articles on multiple websites, blogs, and other online media channels.

As devoted Christians and members of The Church of Jesus Christ of Latter-day Saints, Aaron and April believe that marriage is ordained by God and that He has all the answers to creating "happily ever after." As the parents of three rambunctious little boys, they enjoy family time, college football, long drives, yummy food, and romantic getaways.